World Food

CALIFORNIA

Richard Sterling

WORLD FOOD California
1st edition – May 2003

Published by Lonely Planet Publications Pty Ltd ABN 36 005 607 983

Lonely Planet Offices
Australia Locked Bag 1, Footscray, Victoria 3011
USA 150 Linden Street, Oakland CA 94607
UK 10a Spring Place, London NW5 3BH
France 1 rue du Dahomey, 75011 Paris

Publishing manager Peter D'Onghia
Commissioning editor Martin Heng & Lyndal Hall
Project manager Bridget Blair
Series design & layout Brendan Dempsey
Editors Joanne Newell, Kyla Gillzan, Meaghan Amor
Mapping Natasha Velleley
Photography Jerry Alexander, except images on pages 148–149 by Garrett Culhane

Photography
Many of the photographs in this book are available for licensing from
Lonely Planet Images: www.lonelyplanetimages.com

Front cover – Cabernet Sauvignon grapes
Back cover – Loma doing Yoga

ISBN 1 74059 430 4

text & maps © Lonely Planet Publications Pty Ltd, 2003
photos © photographers as indicated 2003

Printed by H & Y Printing Ltd
Printed in Hong Kong

10 9 8 7 6 5 4 3 2 1

MAP KEY

Place to Eat & Drink	Freeway	State Capital
Building	Primary Road	Town
Plaza Square	Secondary Road	Church
Campus	Tertiary Road	Museum
Cemetery	Tunnel	Monument
Park, Garden	Railway, Station	Stately Home
Sports Ground	Cable Car, Station	Route Numbers
	Metro, Station	

About the Author

Richard Sterling is known as the Indiana Jones of Gastronomy for his willingness to go anywhere and court any danger for the sake of a good meal. His other books include *Greece, Hong Kong, Spain* and *Vietnam* for Lonely Planet's *World Food* series; *The Fire Never Dies*; *Dining with Headhunters*; *The Fearless Diner*; and the award-winning *Travelers' Tales: A Taste of the Road*. He has been honoured by the James Beard Foundation for his food writing, and by Lowell Thomas awards for his travel literature. His lifestyle column "Maitre d" appears monthly in *San Francisco* magazine. Though he lives in Berkeley, California, he is very often politically incorrect.

Richard wishes to thank: Garrett Culhane for his able assistance and advice, Gina Comaich for her encouragement and inspiration, Laurie Armstrong just for being Laurie Armstrong, Brian Reccow for the beer, Jerry Alexander for the wine, Robert Berend for the great party, James O'Reilly and Larry Habegger for always believing in me in spite of all, Bruce Harmon for replacing my differential, Therese Harmon for the stuffed potatoes (damn, they were good!), Laurie "Natasha" Pappas for her espionage, the crew of Amtrak's Coast Starlight for making California even more wonderful, and to the UC Berkeley football team for finally winning back the axe. Go Bears! And to those most agreeable nieces Brittany, Laura and Kyley I send a conk on the noggin and a noogie.

About the Photographer

Jerry Alexander is a highly credited food and travel photographer with extensive experience working in Southeast Asia, particularly Thailand. When he's not traveling around the world – leaving behind a trail of crumbs from eating his props – Jerry lives in California and tends to his vineyard in the Napa Valley. Jerry was the main photographer for *Caribbean, Mexico* and *Thailand* in Lonely Planet's *World Food* series.

From Jerry: Those of us who make images for a living know we seldom do it without help. California is my home and as I traveled from the north to the south I was constantly reminded of what a special home it is. To all who helped me bring life to this book I'm most grateful. It was a wonderful experience. A special thanks to my wife Loma who always brings light to my life.

From the Publisher

This first edition of *World Food California* was commissioned by Martin Heng and Lyndal Hall, edited by Joanne Newell, Kyla Gillzan and Meaghan Amor, and designed by Brendan Dempsey. Natasha Velleley mapped. Bridget Blair, project manager, oversaw the book's production, while Peter D'Onghia, publishing manager, dealt with big picture issues. Thanks to Lonely Planet Images for coordinating the supply of photographs, and for captioning, cataloguing and pre-press work.

UPDATES & READERS FEEDBACK

Things change – prices go up, schedules change, good places go bad and bad places go bankrupt. Nothing stays the same. So, if you find things better or worse, recently opened or long-since closed, please tell us and help make the next edition even more accurate and useful.

Lonely Planet thoroughly updates each guidebook as often as possible – usually every two years, although for some destinations the gap can be longer. Between editions, up-to-date information is available in our free, quarterly Planet Talk newsletter and monthly email bulletin Comet. The Upgrades section of our website (w www.lonelyplanet.com) is also regularly updated by Lonely Planet authors, and the site's Scoop section covers news and current affairs relevant to travellers. Lastly, the Thorn Tree bulletin board and Postcards section carry unverified, but fascinating, reports from travelers.

Tell us about it! We genuinely value your feedback. A well-traveled team at Lonely Planet reads and acknowledges every email and letter we receive and ensures that every morsel of information finds its way to the relevant authors, editors, and cartographers.

Everyone who writes to us will find their name listed in the next edition of the appropriate guidebook, and will receive the latest issue of Comet or Planet Talk. The very best contributions will be rewarded with a free guidebook.

We may edit, reproduce, and incorporate your comments in Lonely Planet products such as guidebooks, websites, and digital products, so let us know if you don't want your comments reproduced or your name acknowledged.

How to contact Lonely Planet:
On-line: e talk2us@lonelyplanet.com.au, w www.lonelyplanet.com
Australia: Locked Bag 1, Footscray, Victoria 3011
UK: 10a Spring Place, London NW5 3BH
USA: 150 Linden St, Oakland, CA 94607

Introduction 8

The Culture of California Cuisine 9
History 10
Geography 18
How Californians Eat 21

Staples & Specialties 31
Vegetables 33
Fruits & Nuts 48
Meat, Fish & Fowl 53
Cheese 69
Bread 73
Olives & Oil 77
Sweets 78

Drinks 81
Wine 82
Beer 105
Cocktails 109
Non-Alcoholic Drinks 116

Home Cooking 121
Taco 125
Chop Suey 126

Celebrating with Food 127
Celebratory Food 129
Harvest Festivals 133

Regional Variations 137
Northern California 139
Southern California 150
La Frontera (The Frontier) 164
The Road 165

171 **Shopping & Markets**
174 Farmers' Markets
178 Things to Take Home

181 **Where to Eat & Drink**
183 Where to Eat
193 Where to Drink
203 Vegetarians & Vegans

205 **A Californian Banquet**

213 **Index**

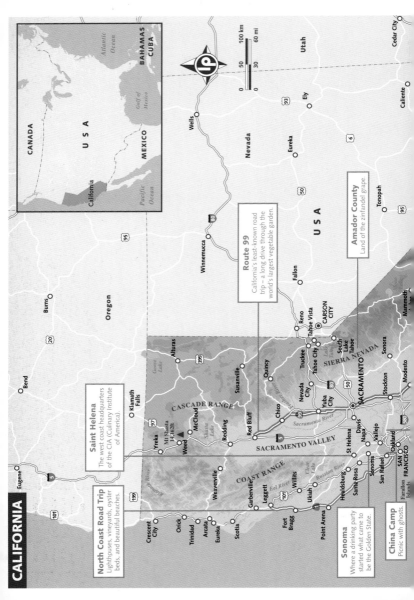

CALIFORNIA

North Coast Road Trip
Lighthouses, vineyards, oyster beds, and beautiful beaches.

Saint Helena
The west coast headquarters of the CIA (Culinary Institute of America).

Route 99
California's least-known road trip – a long drive through the world's largest vegetable garden.

Amador County
Land of the zinfandel grape.

Sonoma
Where a drinking party started what came to be the Golden State.

China Camp
Picnic with ghosts.

100 km
60 mi

CANADA
U S A
MEXICO
Atlantic Ocean
Pacific Ocean
Gulf of Mexico
BAHAMAS
CUBA
California

Oregon
Nevada
Utah

Burns
Bend
Wells
Winnemucca
Fallon
Reno
CARSON CITY
Tahoe Vista
Ely
Eureka
Cedar City
Caliente
Tonopah

Eugene
Crescent City
Orick
Trinidad
Arcata
Eureka
Scotia
Fort Bragg
Point Arena
Leggett
Garberville
Willits
Ukiah
Healdsburg
Santa Rosa
Sonoma
San Rafael
SAN FRANCISCO
Oakland
Vallejo
Napa
St Helena
Davis
SACRAMENTO
Stockton
Modesto
Sonora
South Lake Tahoe
Truckee
Tahoe City
Nevada City
Yuba City
Chico
Red Bluff
Redding
Weed
Yreka
Klamath Falls
McCloud
Weaverville
Susanville
Quincy
Alturas

Farallon Islands
Mammoth Lakes

CASCADE RANGE
COAST RANGE
SIERRA NEVADA
SACRAMENTO VALLEY

Mt Shasta 14,162ft
Shasta Lake
Clear Lake
Goose Lake
Sacramento River
Russian River
Eel River
Klamath River

20
95
5
199
101
101
97
395
80
50
50
6
93
95
99

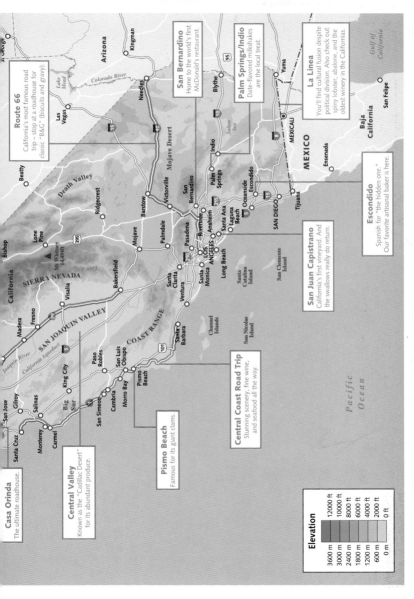

Route 66
California's most famous road trip – stop at a roadhouse for classic "B&G" (biscuits and gravy).

San Bernardino
Home to the world's first McDonald's restaurant.

Palm Springs/Indio
Date-flavored milkshakes are the local treat.

La Linea
You'll find cultural fusion despite political division. Also check out spiny lobster, abalone, and the oldest winery in the Californias.

Escondido
Spanish for "the hidden one." Our favorite artisanal baker is here.

San Juan Capistrano
California's first vineyard. And the swallows really do return.

Central Coast Road Trip
Stunning scenery, fine wine, and seafood all the way.

Pismo Beach
Famous for its giant clams.

Central Valley
Known as the "Cadillac Desert" for its abundant produce.

Casa Orinda
The ultimate roadhouse.

Elevation

3600 m	12000 ft
3000 m	10000 ft
2400 m	8000 ft
1800 m	6000 ft
1200 m	4000 ft
600 m	2000 ft
0 m	0 ft

"California Cuisine" is justifiably famous throughout the culinary world. Take the finest, freshest ingredients available on the planet and interfere with them as little as possible, just enough to make them sing in your mouth. Serve them up with the superior Californian wine, artisanal bread and cheese, and large measures of Californian panache and sunshine. Who could withhold praise?

California's world-famous cities of San Francisco and Los Angeles, and the almost legendary Napa Valley, are the best-known symbols of this magical place. In those places the food and drink are of a caliber as high as the world's best. But it doesn't stop there. That isn't the sum of California's "gold." This state is the birthplace of North America's only indigenous beer-brewing style; the font of its emerging coffee culture; the center for fine tea; and a great place for a steak. California's lesser-known Central Valley sets the world's prices for commodity crops, ranging from almonds to zinfandel grapes. And the only place you'll find more Asian restaurants is in, well, Asia! San Francisco is the cultural capital of the western USA, and Los Angeles is the capital of the Pacific Rim – all those nations of the PacRim bring their culinary offerings to the City of Angels, just as the western Americans look to Baghdad by the Bay and think of delicious things to eat.

Mexico has been in California's gastronomic soul since 1769. Cal-Mex cuisine is immediately recognizable as being of Mexican origin, as well as being immediately, recognizably, not Mexican. Chop suey also comes from California, and you'll never find it in China. That's why they say "as American as chop suey." And of course the Californians invented fast-food, but it's considered impolite to remind them of that.

the culture of
california cuisine

As with other aspects of Californian culture, the cuisine of California is easy to recognize and hard to define, partly because it's always in flux, always reinventing itself. In California the only thing that stays the same is change. But you can be sure that no matter the times or fortunes, Californians will be eating and drinking with gusto. They like to think they invented gusto. Maybe they did.

History

California is a land of the imagination. Even the name of the "Golden State" sprang from the imagination, a fiction – a novel, to be precise. In the year 1510 Garcia Ordoñez de Montalvo, the Spanish writer of chivalrous romances, published *The Adventures of Esplandian*, whose hero learns of a far-off land ruled by a beautiful woman called Califia, for whom the kingdom is named.

> *Know that on the right hand of the Indies there is an island called California very close to the side of the Terrestrial Paradise; and it is peopled by black women, without any man among them, for they live in the manner of Amazons. They are of strong and hardy bodies, of ardent courage, and great force. Their island is the strongest in the world, with its steep cliffs and rock shores. Their arms are of gold, and so is the harness of the wild beasts they tame to ride, for in the whole island there is no metal but gold.*

California's own troubadours, The Beach Boys, would surely approve of these original California Girls.

Geographically, California is composed of several distinct regions – the US territory of Alta (Upper) California, and the Mexican territories of Baja (Lower) California Norte (North) and Baja California Sur (South). From there the Spanish, through the efforts and imagination of their mission-aries, steadily expanded their writ northward, building a string of mutually supporting missions along a mule track that came to be known as El Camino Real, or The King's Highway. When it reached Alta California in 1769, the Spaniards, under the spiritual leadership of Father Junipero Serra, found the local inhabitants to be hunter-gatherers who lived chiefly on game and acorns, and liked it just fine. In their manner of dress Father Serra wrote that these heathen men "go as naked as Adam before the fall." He hurried to provide them with trousers, the word of God, and the astounding news that there was a place called Hell.

Plumbjack vineyards in early summer, Napa Valley

The missionaries quickly planted what crops they had brought: wheat, corn (maize), beans, figs, grapes, and a few garden vegetables. Over time they also introduced olives and domesticated animals, mainly pigs and poultry. Over the 500-mile length of the mission chain in Alta California the diet was wholesome but plain. The daily fare was a maize porridge called *pozole*.

Civilian Spaniard settlers, known as Californios, followed in the wake of the missions. They raised cattle, sheep, goats, and pigs. They farmed a bit. They hunted the sea otter and traded its pelt for manufactured items brought by the ships of "Yankee traders" from New England on the American Atlantic coast. They established enormous *ranchos*, agricultural enterprises usually given to cattle raising. The hides and tallow of the cattle also went mainly to the Yankee traders. On feast days they enjoyed the fandango, basically a barbecue with music, dancing, and amorous goings-on. Many a lady's ankle might be seen at such boisterous affairs. In 1822 Mexico gained independence from Spain, but little changed in quiet California, for this was its pastoral age.

In 1846 a ragtag group of mostly American adventurers got drunk in the little town of Sonoma at the end of the mission trail, and imagined themselves as nation builders. They seized the government, which at that time was led by General Mariano Vallejo, and declared an independent republic. A brief war between the USA and Mexico ensued. In 1847 the argument was settled and California went over to the USA. In 1848 gold was discovered along the Sacramento River. Life would never be the same. The many thousands who converged on California during 1848 and 1849, each eager for their piece of gold, were referred to as 49ers.

Roughing It

It was that population that gave to California a name for getting up astounding enterprises and rushing them through with a magnificent dash and daring and a recklessness of cost or consequences, which she bears unto this day – and when she projects a new enterprise, the grave world smiles as usual and says, "Well, that is California all over."

Mark Twain, Roughing It, *1872*

Immigration now contributed to California's gastronomy. People from all over the world, suddenly and in great numbers, converged on this place. They brought with them their very different customs, traditions, and tastes, and ways of living and eating. In an instant, the population was exposed to *other* ideas. It was like going to live at the World's Fair. It is important to remember that Californians have always tended to be immigrants, and still are, even today. They might be from the neighboring progressive state of Oregon, or maybe from India. But

Adobe communal oven at Mission San Francisco de Solano, Sonoma

half of Californians have come from somewhere else. What makes them alike is what they do when they get here. And just like the native-born, they eventually become the cultural and historical heirs of those original Spanish/Mexican Californios.

For nearly 100 years things of culinary interest would center mainly on San Francisco and its surrounds. There in the cosmopolitan city, with the nearby wine growing region and natural abundance of food, people ate and drank with gusto and sometimes wrote about it. After the Anglo-American meat-and-potatoes variety of cooking, the most important influences were Chinese, Mexican and, especially, Italian. Every town of any size in California, from those days to the present, has had at least one Italian restaurant. And most have had Chinese or Mexican restaurants, or both. These places are still as much a part of California's culinary landscape as that style the world has come to call California Cuisine (see California Cuisine, p21).

By the mid-20th century imagination had made California a land of vast wealth – in gold and silver, in agriculture, in Hollywood dreams, and in Disney fantasies. There was much that was good to eat and drink, but there was also much that was rather dull. The natural foods of field and stream were superb, fruits and vegetables of the highest repute. But still many people did not think much about what they ate or how to eat it. And if they did, they all too often looked to Europe for what to do. Then came M. F. K. (Mary Frances Kennedy) Fisher. She was from the southern Californian town of Whittier. Her family's kitchen had always been a happy place, and in her youth she had lived and studied much in France. She was not a cook, but a writer. And it was she who can be said to have invented modern American food writing. Indeed, she elevated it to the realm of literature.

Lumber mill, northern California

Fisher's near contemporaries continued to lay the groundwork for what was to come. James Beard, considered to be the dean of American gastronomy in his time, began to wean himself away from New York and France and spend time in California. Julia Child was educating the nation in cookery, albeit in a rather Frenchified way, and nowhere in the USA had more cookery students than California. The nouvelle cuisine of France had Californian cooks thinking and talking. They talked about the fact that their menus tended to be printed in French. That they would not be taken seriously if they didn't include certain canonical foods such as foie gras, sole, and canard a l'orange, no matter that they came to the house in a can or frozen, and bore no relation whatever to the place and people of California. Their conversations were reflected in newspaper columns and in home kitchens. The stage was being set for culinary change, and without the willing consumer, the provider would be as nothing. Or as Emerson, America's original man of letters wrote, "'Tis the good reader makes the good book."

Faces of Gastronomy – M. F. K. FISHER

Mary Frances Kennedy Fisher often organized her essays around food, around hunger and our various struggles towards its satisfaction, and the goodness we find along the way. But she was not a cookbook author or a food writer in the traditional sense. She did not write of food, literally, but of food as an evocation of place and time and memory, and of sharing its pleasures amid myriad difficulties.

American food writers owe Fisher an enormous debt; more than any other writer in this language, she tossed out the tenants of Puritanism and wrote about the senses, about engaging with life, in a way still foreign to most people of Anglo-Saxon decent. She nearly single-handedly, and perhaps entirely unintentionally, eclipsed the domestic scientists who had such a grip on our appetites at the dawn of the 20th century. She wrote about being a human animal with hungers and fears and passions and deeper desires, and she did so with an unflinchingly honest eye, a deliciously sensual ethic, and a phenomenal command of the English language.

Michelle Anna Jordan, author and radio host, Santa Rosa

Mary Frances Kennedy Fisher (left) and Michelle Anna Jordan

Through the 1960s the nation was in a ferment of change, especially in California, and most especially in the university town of Berkeley, across the bay from San Francisco. Many were imagining a world revolution. But others were imagining good things to eat and good ways to eat them. In 1971 a young woman named Alice Waters, an immigrant from the garden state of New Jersey, opened a restaurant in a converted house near the University of California in Berkeley. She called it Chez Panisse, after a fictional character in a romantic novel. Her purpose was not to change the world, but to use some of the techniques of French cookery, with a bit of California home-kitchen craft, to make the best of what was available locally, seasonally and naturally. She imagined that if she could bring out the entire range of possibility of something as simple and ordinary as a ripe tomato or a stalk of asparagus, she could "shock with the familiar."

It was breathtakingly simple. And still is.

Harvest time is family time in California

A MATTER OF CONVENIENCE

To its credit or its shame, California is the birthplace of the drive-thru restaurant, the supermarket, and fast food. The state's first supermarket was Ralph's in Los Angeles, appearing in the 1920s. Fast food came about shortly after WWII, when American society was on the move with an enormous and sustained burst of energy. Massive road building projects were under way, especially in California; cars were produced in record numbers; and food production soared with mechanized farming. People were always on the go, always pressed for time. In 1948, brothers Mac and Dick MacDonald opened their first self-serve (waiterless) burger joint in San Bernardino, just outside LA. Later that year and just down the road, the Snyder family opened the first In-N-Out Burger drive-thru restaurant. And the supermarket, from it's small beginnings 20 years previously, came into its own. The rest is history.

It is trite to say that these food retailers have become institutions, and it is equally trite to say that social critics blame them for many social ills. In California in the '60s and '70s their chief complaint was that this industrialization of the acts of nourishment had caused a divorce between production and consumption, between the nourishment and the nourished. Industrial food had become bland and robbed of much of its value, and people had forgotten what things should or could taste like. Eating was no longer an act of communion between the eater and the natural world. It was reduced to mere necessity. Many Californians listened closely to these arguments, and in so doing, prepared the ground for those who would make the changes soon to come.

It's not all fancy food in the Golden State

Geography

Geography is fate both in politics and provender, and nowhere more than in California. The Golden State has every kind of climate except tropical rainforest. It can and does grow virtually every kind of food crop, and in huge abundance. It comprises the world's seventh largest economy, with agriculture its biggest industry. That industry is mainly focused on what is known as the Central Valley. California could be described as an ellipse of mountains surrounding the world's widest, longest, flattest pan of deep alluvial soil. The northern half, known as the Sacramento, is well watered. The southern half, known as the San Joaquin, is arid. But in the early 20th century work began to harness the Colorado and Sacramento Rivers and channel their waters to the valley where they say they "made the desert bloom." It became known as the Cadillac Desert, after America's original luxury car.

Sierra Nevada mountain meadow

Setting sun off the Californian coast

CENTRAL VALLEY NATIVE SON

It is a land of rubes, of hardworking people, of immigrants from all over the world. It is the land the urbane folks tend to forget, if not outright disdain, as a hot or foggy interruption, pending the time of year, en route to somewhere else. LA or Tahoe, perhaps, as the bunched up coastal people prefer. It is the defining aspect of what California is: "a long central valley encircled by mountains," writes geographer John Crow. And geography is key. The cuisine of France or Italy may be about culture. But in California, cuisine is about geography, about living in a land of inexpressible fertility.

The Central Valley is the quiet superlative where seemingly everything is grown, or is produced, at its utmost. Milk. Cotton. Walnuts. Almonds. Peaches. Tomatoes. And the list goes on. A land where each farmer feeds more than 80 people. It is a vast trough consisting of 15 million acres.

And unto this big land came the need for big equipment. The Fresno scraper, the basic design for giant earthmovers; the Stockton gangplow for tilling huge swaths of land; the Caterpillar track-type tractors; the tomato harvester; the mechanical grape harvester; the rotary orchard pruner; the cruise stacker for alfalfa; the tree shaker and sweeper for nut harvesting – all born out of necessity in the great Central Valley.

It is a place of geometric intrigue. First the daunting plain, that from the center, where the many rivers converge to form the delta, rises so imperceptibly that it can be measured only by laser. The pristine linear rows of tomatoes, tracts of almond and peach orchards, tender vines of grapes trellised, campestral grassland, winding asphalt roads atop former stagecoach routes, and the columns of Washingtonia or Canary Island palms that, like sentries, so often line the entrances to the older farms and ranches that grace the valley. The checkerboard of rotating crops. The rows of rusting vehicles and antiquated farm equipment that invariably gather in the farmers' yards. The gentle curves of aqueducts carrying water to the thirsty lands of Southern California. The canals that diagonally dissect the fertile fields. The meandering of rivers flush from the Sierra snowpack, the adjacent riparian woods, and floodplains at some points stretching a dozen miles wide.

It is a place of contrasts, particularly along the fringes of the valley, where a few hundred yards can make the difference between soil suitable for an orchard, or that best left to pasture. Or the very heart, the loamy delta, a land so rich one doesn't grow food but seed for food to be planted elsewhere in the grain belts of the world. The delta is, in essence, a petri dish, one huge laboratory of dark, fertile soil. That is my native Central Valley.

Garrett Culhane was lead photographer for World Food Vietnam

How Californians Eat
California Cuisine

What people call "California Cuisine" is not a canon of recipes. It is a goal. That goal is to bring the best of the local environment to the table, its integrity intact and in season, and prepared with a light touch. The cooking techniques and tools and kitchen craft are informed chiefly by the Mediterranean styles of southern France and northern Italy, whose climate and soil are remarkably similar to California's. It is often called "ingredient driven," but that is not to say that certain ingredients are required or that others are banned. It is so called because the greatest attention is paid to the production and procurement of the finest ingredients possible. Freshness is an obsession. And in the preparation, the "freshness speaks for itself," says Alice Waters of Chez Panisse. In other words, a dish is only as good as its ingredients.

Olive oil is a favored cooking medium, but by no means the only one. If the local environment produced only yak butter and tulip bulbs the Californian chef would get the best of them and make you a tasty dish. Sauces are not frowned upon, but neither are they emphasized. And they are never heavy or copious. Vinaigrettes are more common, as are reductions of stock and wine. Meat is by no means shunned, but there is an emphasis on fruits and vegetables, which are lightly cooked, and interfered with as little as possible. A common dish is snow peas or sugar-snap peas (with edible pods) tossed in a pan, or even a wok, with extra virgin olive oil, and perhaps a drop of balsamic vinegar, splash of white wine, or dusting of pepper. The chef will not rely on a cookbook to determine what seasonings to use, or their quantities, but on the balance of sugars, aromas, crispness, and color of that particular batch of beautiful green pods. Bringing out those always-changing qualities is a practice of improvisation that Alice Waters compares to jazz music. And it is the essence of California Cuisine. Edible jazz.

To ensure a steady supply of ingredients, virtually all California Cuisine restaurants maintain close relations with as many of their suppliers as possible. Most fruits and vegetables come from small family farms, sometimes called "boutique" farms. They are for the most part local, organic farms practicing sustainable agriculture. Cheeses, breads and meats are provided by local artisans. At Chez Panisse, Waters established the position of forager, where a person's sole duty is to scour the land for fine ingredients. Others have followed this example.

The lodestar Chez Panisse has thrown off many bright sparks, and inspired many imitators. The Austrian chef Wolfgang Puck saw the possibilities, moved to Los Angeles and opened Spago restaurant. He became not merely a celebrity but an industry unto himself, with a line of frozen

As California's anthem goes, "bowers of flowers bloom in the sun," and these are edible!

and packed foods that command high prices in supermarkets. Michael McCarty came from his training in France to Santa Monica where he was able to serve food that was "green and crunchy instead of brown and mushy." The alumni of Chez Panisse are too many to list but include Jeremiah Tower, who opened the famous Stars Restaurant in San Francisco; Paul Bertolli, now of Oliveto in Oakland; Peggy Smith, at Cowgirl Creamery in Marin; and Mark Miller, who took his experience to New Mexico where he opened the famous Coyote Cafe, serving the increasingly popular Southwestern cuisine.

Alice Waters in the kitchen of Chez Panisse, Berkeley

California Cuisine keeps evolving in its endless edible jazz riff. And it spins off into other styles, practices and ideas. Pacific Rim cuisine (PacRim) is one of them. This is a Californian exploration into the seductions of East Asia. But the climate and soil are different, and herbs will never be the same on both sides of the Pacific. So chefs have taken the California Cuisine credo of making the most of the locality. Chef Charles Hechinger of the Pacific restaurant in San Francisco is one of its practitioners. "It's not fusion cuisine," he says. "It's like a galaxy of dishes from those Asian communities here in California. We try to stay true to the original, but know we can't, so we don't mind using a little olive oil, a dash of wine. Although we don't always recommend drinking wine with PacRim. The flavors in a meal are often too various. Beer is good. If the bar menu is PacRim then a martini is good. There is one wine, now I think of it – champagne goes well with all."

Etiquette

Though American children are often instructed to not put their elbows on the table, everyone gets away with it in California. General table manners are fairly intuitive – don't chew with your mouth open, or speak in a loud voice, or behave in a rude manner, and you'll be OK. You should also wait until everyone is served before starting to eat. At the beginning of a meal it's good form to offer a companion a taste of your dish. Should they accept, simply cut off a small piece and put it on his or her plate. Table servers are politely addressed as "waiter," not "sir" or "miss," "buddy," or "hey, you!"

In general, Americans tend to be "fork-shifters." They hold the fork straight up in the left hand, with the tines down, often with fingers splayed out, then saw away with the knife in the right hand. Then they set the knife down, shift the empty fork to the right hand, tines up, and spear or scoop the food and carry it to the mouth. Then they shift back and start the whole cumbersome business over again. Why do they go through so much wasted motion? In early colonial times manufactured items were in short supply, especially among the common folk. The kitchen and dining facilities of the early colonial home were basically those of a primitive camp. Serving vessels, for example, were virtually nonexistent. And even such ordinary necessities as drinking vessels might be in too short supply to allot one to each member of a household. The same went for table knives. So the custom arose of cutting meat with the right hand then passing the knife on to one's neighbor, and picking up the fork, again with the right hand, to eat. It might have lent a measure of conviviality to the table, but it was surely distracting.

Eating Out
Reservations (Bookings)

It's always a good idea to secure a table ahead of time. Even if that time is as little as a few hours. There are a few restaurants that don't take reservations, but will allow you to call ahead to be put on the waiting list an hour ahead of time. This means you should be able to avoid waiting outside. But by and large, a proper sit-down restaurant will be happy to reserve a table for you. If it's on the A-list, a must-go-to, see-and-be-seen sort of place, you may have to wait weeks for that reservation, but they will make it for you.

In recent years the reservations process has become irksome at many of the more high-profile establishments. It can be next to impossible to speak to a human being when you call. You will be answered by a recording that will give you an eight-item menu of buttons to push, each of which will direct you to another set of options. In the end you'll leave your name, contact info, and a time and date request, and hope for the best. They might get back to you with a confirmation, they might not. If they don't, we suggest that you give them a miss. We don't like to reward bad behavior.

CULTURE

Jeanty at Jack's, a gold rush legacy in San Francisco

On the other hand, there is often bad behavior on the part of patrons. There is a plague of people who call for a table and then don't show up. This kind of behavior has a direct and immediate economic impact on an enterprise that operates on a very thin profit margin. In self-defense, many have taken to requiring a credit card deposit in order to secure a reservation. A typical deposit might be $25 to $50 for the table. If you cancel after the restaurant's deadline, usually 24 to 48 hours in advance of your reserved time, you forfeit the deposit.

When making reservations at a popular venue it's wise to be flexible. When you call you may be told that you can only be seated very early or very late. In SoCal (Southern California) late is always easier to book, and in NorCal (Northern California) early is usually easier to book. Many restaurants may be booked on-line these days. Just log on, see what's available at the place of your choice, and claim it.

Valet Parking

How easy, convenient, and even luxurious it all is. Drive up to the restaurant's entrance, toss your keys to the parking valet, and forget about the pain of parking, getting lost, or having to park so far away that you need a taxi to carry you to and from the restaurant. No need to walk through mean streets, asphalt jungles, or past sellers of tourist junk and knickknacks, or autographed pictures of Hollywood stars. Hurrah for the valet parkers!

Silverado Resort and Spa, Napa Valley

The valet situation is best in SoCal, and best of all in LA. This is the city designed for the automobile. Parking is plentiful, so the valet function is, really, more an affectation than a genuine convenience. It's also cheap – $3 to $5 gets you parked securely, and upon exiting the establishment your coach awaits. NorCal, especially in San Francisco, is different. Here, the valet parker can be as essential to good dining as a timely reservation. The average cost is $10, and if you have ever had to take up the parking challenge in San Francisco, you'll pay it gladly. But north or south, remember to tip your parker. They are paid a very small wage and so depend on tips for their livelihood. A tip of $2 is not over the top; $3 is better.

Incidentals

Trying to avoid a corkage fee? How about cuttage? On occasion, patrons like to bring their own specially made cakes for birthday dinners. Traditionally this has never been a problem, and restaurants have always been happy to accommodate. Lately, however, certain chichi joints up and down the state have been levying a tax on this kind of celebrating. They charge, per diner, to cut the damned thing. Even if it's already cut! Perhaps in the future they'll charge a lightage fee for igniting the candles. And then a blowage fee. Call ahead and ask.

Bottled water is all the rage. It started in the 1980s when Perrier of France began to convince Americans that they should drink a beverage that tastes a lot like club soda but comes in a green bottle and costs a lot of green. Now there are any number of designer waters from which to choose. If bottled water is your cup of tea, that's fine. Order it. But be warned that you can pay up to $10 per liter in the swankier joints. Most places, however, offer a very serviceable iced tea, costing a pittance, made from tap water, and they will refill your glass endlessly at no extra charge.

Smoking

Most books in the Lonely Planet World Food series warn the reader that locals might smoke at the table. In most of Europe and Asia people think nothing of igniting a big fat cigar and holding it under your nose as you try to dine. If this bothers you, then you are heading to No Nicotine Nirvana. At the end of the 20th century the Californian legislature banned smoking in all restaurants and most bars throughout the state. Where food is served within the Governor's writ, smoking is forbidden. In a bar, smoking may be permitted if the establishment is operated directly by the owner and family members. The basis of this law is one of workers' rights. Employers may not endanger the health of employees by exposing them to secondhand smoke. They may endanger their patrons and themselves, but not their employees.

GETTING TIPSY

We generally don't mind a fixed gratuity when a restaurant's staff pushes in our chairs, clandestinely refolds our napkins, and acts in the manner of a waiter at Paris' Alain Ducasse, where, a friend remarks, she was all but offered cupped hands when she needed to use the ladies' room. But what happens if we believe the included tip isn't deserved?

San Francisco's Cosmopolitan Café requires an 18% gratuity for parties of more than eight. But co-owner Christian Corbett promises, "If a party is not satisfied with the service, we do whatever it takes to make sure they leave smiling." At Farallon, which charges 18% for parties of seven or more, general manager Tyler Williams admits, "In the past year and a half, I've seen three tables have problems. When I presented the bill, I told them the set fee was waived and to use their discretion when tipping." We expect restaurants to take the approach of the customer is always right with unhappy diners.

Farallon, San Francisco

Common Cents
The restaurant industry is structured so that waiters need to get good tips just to make a living. Unbeknownst to the average diner, a tip is usually divided among up to 10 restaurant employees. Waiters distribute anywhere from 30% to 50% of their tips to hostesses, bartenders, sommeliers, and food runners. Despite the handouts, waiters are still required to claim 8% of their total sales as tips come tax time, so when the math is done, a less-than-15% perk could mean out-of-pocket payments for an under-earning waiter.

Fair Pay
Still, it's our right to decide how much we think a waiter's job is worth. When we're satisfied, it's only fair to stick to tipping the industry standard: at least 15% of the total bill for good service [20% in LA], closer to 17% in fine dining rooms, 20% for great service anywhere, and additional antes for special treatment or unexpected freebies. Add $1 per hanger for the coat check.

Erika Lenkert, writing in San Francisco Magazine

CULTURE

Dining with Children

A few suggestions.

Go early in NorCal and later in SoCal. Fewer adults will be present to witness any loss of composure.

Call the restaurant ahead of time and ask if there are special menus or recommended dishes for kids, and for any other accommodation such as risers (booster seats) or high chairs. Also ask about the noise level. If it's quiet, think twice.

Drill the little ones in public table manners. Make a serious game of it. Offer bribes for the best conduct befitting a kid.

Authorize the children to do the tipping. Tell them what the scale is and let them act according to their level of satisfaction. Make sure the waiter knows. And make up for any lack.

Fourth of July feast, Napa

CULTURE

CONTINUING EDUCATION

In California you can begin your culinary education in primary school and continue on to advanced degrees. Numerous private cooking schools offer courses for children.

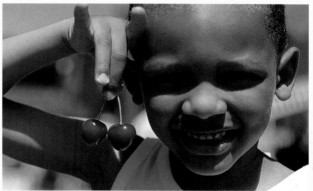

You can't get much better than fresh cherries!

The Sustainable Kitchen in Berkeley teaches primary school kids how to prepare complete, balanced meals and how to have fun doing it. Also emphasized is the concept of sustainable agriculture, reinforced by visits to organic farms. One-day courses make for excellent day care.

w *www.sustainablekitchen.com*

Also in Berkeley, Alice Waters has created the educational program known as the **Edible Schoolyard**, implemented at Martin Luther King Middle School. According to the website, its purpose "is to create and sustain an organic garden and landscape which is wholly integrated into the school's curriculum and lunch program. It involves the students in all aspects of farming the garden – along with preparing, serving and eating the food – as a means of awakening their senses and encouraging awareness and appreciation of the transformative values of nourishment, community, and stewardship of the land." Visitors are welcome by prior arrangement.

w *www.edibleschoolyard.org*

Professional education begins at the **California Culinary Academy** in San Francisco where full-time students earn post-secondary degrees in culinary arts, restaurant management, baking, and pastry. The Academy, at 625 Polk Street, also has two full-service restaurants operated by the students. When you dine there you're eating the results of their classes. The food usually gets an A from diners, and the cost is generally lower than comparable restaurants. The institution even has a television series called *Cooking at the Academy*, which airs on public television.

W *www.baychef.com*

Postgraduate studies take place at the **CIA** (Culinary Institute of America) in Saint Helena. While the main focus is on professional development in all aspects of food and wine service, many lectures and demonstrations are open to the public. There is a superb restaurant, a large bookstore, and a gift shop. Located in the beautiful stone winery formerly owned by The Christian Brothers, it should be included in any visit to the Napa Valley.

W *www.ciachef.edu*

For an outdoor educational experience, check the calendar of **Earthbound Farm**. Here you can take a tour of the nation's first commercial organic farm, participate in the harvest, hear a lecture on wine, or learn how to braid garlic. The Farm Stand is located at 7250 Carmel Valley Road, Carmel (3.5 miles east of Highway 1).

W *www.ebfarm.com*

staples
& specialties

How does one determine the staple foods and regional specialties for a place that grows – and eats – everything? And we do mean everything. California is the world on a plate. Since 1848 the entire globe has come to California, to get rich, make new lives, and seek, bring, or create the new and unusual.

Abundant harvest of corn

What are the foods of California? The easier question is, what are not? Well, no one eats penguin, or human flesh, as far as we know. Marmite and Vegemite have never made inroads here. So what is the secret? While we can say that Californians eat virtually everything, that is not the complete answer. It is in how they eat everything. It is in their passion, their curiosity, their love and zest for everything. It is in how they experience everything.

Vegetables

Californians have every vegetable you can imagine available to them. And they use them all. There is nothing that grows in the ground that they do not eat. And when they tire of these crops, their botanists invent new ones for them to grow and enjoy. The Golden State provides the nation with almost all its tomatoes, all its artichokes, lots of its lettuce, scads of its cabbage, and much of all else. The list goes on. You name it, California grows it and sends it out to the rest of the coun-

Zucchini and yellow squash

try. It's that simple. Californians love raw, or slightly blanched, vegetables as a snack or side dish. An arrangement of mixed, blanched vegetables with a dipping sauce or two is a popular party treat, usually called a crudité or vegetable medley. They bake vegetables, they grill vegetables, they boil them, broil them, and eat 'em with potatoes, rice, or tomatoes. But probably the single most common way to take vegetables in California is in a salad.

STAPLES

LETTUCE MESCALUN MIX

Salad

Almost any time is a great time of year for leafy greens, luscious tomatoes, fragrant onions, and just about any other kind of foliage that can be tossed with oil and vinegar. Californians are silly for salad. And why not? They grow the stuff right here. And while the rest of the country is taking lessons from California, it was not always so, at least in the heartland. In the previous generation, salad was thought of as "rabbit food" by many a Yankee. Men of Illinois looked at men of California and considered their eating of salads as evidence of ... um ... a certain sexual persuasion. Thirty years ago journalists and food writers were remarking that in California, even truck drivers were seen eating salad, in public, and that it was not considered notorious.

Cataluna salad, ThirstyBear, San Francisco

Caesar Salad

Perhaps the most famous salad in California, indeed all of America, is the Caesar salad. This is definitely a Californian recipe. Baja California, that is. From La Frontera (see p161). Caesar Cardini was the proprietor of his eponymous restaurant in Tijuana, immediately south of San Diego. During the bad old days of American Prohibition (see p82), when decent folk could not get a decent drink in public, decent folk would descend in droves on Baja California for fun and frolic. They peopled the pubs of

Baby greens at Forni-Brown Gardens, Calistoga

Tijuana, they crowded the cantinas of Ensenada, they roosted in the restaurants of both.

According to those in the know, supplies in the Cardini eatery ran short one busy night in 1924. It was near closing time when a troupe of Norteamericano revelers arrived famished from their exertions at the local casinos, bars, and "houses of one-night wives." They demanded sustenance, of which Caesar had little. He had romaine lettuce, a few eggs, some anchovies, and bread that was only good for croutons, along with a few seasonings. He told his head waiter to "Take everything to the table and make a ceremony of preparing it. Let our guests think they're having the specialty of the house." It just so happened that the ingredients available that fateful night were the perfect balance of taste, aroma, and texture. Anything more or less would have been a blight. It was later to be declared "the greatest recipe to originate from the Americas in 50 years" by the International Society of Epicures in Paris.

Caesar Salad

Ingredients

2	heads romaine lettuce, with leaves torn to bits (or not)
2	egg yolks
2	large cloves garlic, pressed
1 tsp	prepared mustard
½ tsp	Worcestershire sauce
4	anchovies or 1 tbs anchovy paste
¾ cup (175mL)	extra virgin olive oil
2 cups	unseasoned croutons
⅓ cup	parmesan cheese, grated
	juice of 1 lemon
	freshly ground pepper
	salt to taste

Wash and dry the romaine. Set aside. In a large wooden bowl, give the egg yolks a good stir with a wooden spoon. Add the garlic, mustard, Worcestershire sauce, and anchovy, then blend thoroughly. Whisk in the oil and lemon. Add the romaine and the remaining ingredients and toss with great aplomb using salad forks or tongs. You might also work in a bit of élan – showmanship would not hurt. Serve with bread and a thin white wine, or beer, or iced tea. This makes a fine lunch or an appetizer at dinner.

Serves 5–6

Caesar salad, Breeze, Los Angeles

Cobb Salad

Ingredients

½	head iceberg lettuce
½	bunch watercress
1	small bunch chicory
½	head romaine lettuce
2	medium-sized tomatoes, peeled, seeded, and chopped
2	breasts of boiled roasting chicken, diced
6	strips crisp bacon, finely chopped
1	avocado, diced
3	hard-boiled eggs, chopped
2 tbs	chopped chives
½ cup	finely grated Roquefort cheese
	Brown Derby dressing (see recipe opposite)

Finely chop the iceberg lettuce, watercress, chicory, and romaine, and layer these in a glass salad bowl, to show the strata (with the iceberg on the bottom). Sprinkle with the tomato. Toss the chicken over the top of the chopped vegetables, and sprinkle the bacon over the chicken. Arrange the avocado around the edge of the salad. Decorate by sprinkling with the eggs, chives, and cheese. Serve with the dressing on the side.

Serves 6 as a side dish, 3 as a meal

Cobb Salad

For some 70 years the Brown Derby was one of the most famous and most beloved restaurants in Hollywood. Like Chasen's restaurant and the Roosevelt Hotel, it was one of those Hollywood haunts where one would give anything to have been a fly on the wall, as so many good times and debaucheries had gone on there.

The Derby began as a simple burgers, dogs, and barbecue joint that was popular with local lesser film industry folk. In 1925 the owner hired Robert Cobb to manage the place, and it wasn't long before the little hat's most famous menu item appeared: a bowl of artfully presented, finely minced ingredients called a Cobb salad. Contrary to popular misconception, it does not include corn cobs.

The creation story relates how Bob Cobb had visited the dentist. Upon reporting for work afterward he was still hurting from the experience, yet his appetite got the better of him. Unable to chew through barbecued food or burgers, he gathered softer foodstuffs and chopped them very fine, so they would be easy to chew.

Though the Derby is no longer, you can still find the salad in places of tradition. But perhaps the most important feature of the Cobb salad is often overlooked: its texture. The ingredients must be very finely chopped so as to render chewing almost unnecessary. The great sensory pleasure of the Cobb salad is in letting it almost melt in your mouth. A mere swirling of the ingredients between the tongue and the palate should suffice to masticate Cobb's creation. Many places offering the Cobb seem unaware of this and will serve you a huge plate of roughly chopped food. Its arrangement is also important. The different ingredients are not tossed, but are laid out in strata, so that each is displayed to best effect.

Brown Derby Dressing

Ingredients

1 cup (250mL)	red wine vinegar	1 tsp	sugar
2½ tbs	salt	1 tbs	ground black pepper
1 tbs	Worcestershire sauce	1 tbs	English mustard
1	clove garlic, chopped	3 cups	olive oil
	juice of ½ lemon		

Blend all the ingredients together and shake well. Use immediately.
Yields 6 cups (1.5L)

Crab Louis

Crab Louis is such a simple dish, and like so many simple things, took some obscure genius to contrive. It is one of the best ways to enjoy the sweet and distinctive Dungeness crab of the Pacific coast. (There is also a shrimp version for regions lacking the Dungeness.) It is little more than fresh cracked crab on a bed of shredded iceberg lettuce, garnished with boiled eggs and tomatoes (both quartered), and gilded with a mayonnaise and chile-sauce dressing. It arrived on the gastronomic scene around the year 1900. No one knows where it first appeared, but early accounts have it being served in that bastion of San Francisco's high society, the Saint Francis Hotel on Union Square, and at the opposite end of Union Square in Solari's restaurant on Maiden Lane. This little alleyway is ironically named, because at the time this is where one might have found the better class of bordello. Solari's sat atop one of them. It would seem, then, that Crab Louis began as food for people looking to satisfy more than one kind of appetite.

> California, more than any other state in the Union, is a country by itself.
>
> *James Bryce,*
> *The American Commonwealth*

Which one is Louis? Crab and lobster at Fishermans Wharf, San Francisco

Artichoke

People have said that it looks like an armadillo, or some other outlandish armored beast. Or they might also complain that, "It's just a damned thistle! You gonna eat a thistle?" Damned right we're gonna eat a thistle! Lots of 'em! How anyone could think artichokes unattractive is a mystery to Californians. They are prized here not just for their delicate earthy flavor and their beautiful shade of green, but for their symmetry and shape, and suitability for still life paintings. Potters often use artichoke motifs – nose around a pottery boutique and you're likely to find serving vessels, cups, and even ashtrays in the shape of artichokes.

Eat a thistle? Yes!

California is the only commercial source of the nation's artichokes, with most of them coming from the area around Castroville. And California is the chief artichoke consumer. It's almost the official state vegetable. At home they are usually eaten in the gloriously messy style: tear off the leaves one at a time, dip them into mayonnaise and scrape the flesh off with your teeth. When all the leaves are eaten and piled up in the middle of the table, scoop out the hairy "choke" and discard it. Then eat the bowl-shaped bottom, full of mayo.

In restaurants, artichokes are usually served in a more tidy fashion. They make an excellent cream soup. Or the chef may cut away the leaves and chokes and lower stem, leaving only the meaty bottom. This might be served as a Castroville specialty – quartered and deep-fried and served with tartar sauce. Or it might be filled with shrimp or cracked crab and dressed with something rich and creamy. Or it might be steamed, sliced, and tossed into a salad. If the restaurant serves whole artichokes, they're likely to be "baby" artichokes. These are the same as the larger "globe" artichokes, but come from the lower part of the plant. Baby artichokes can be eaten whole – they have no chokes or thorns, and the stems are tender. A common way to prepare baby artichokes is to slice them in two lengthwise and sauté them in olive oil and garlic. Artichokes are generally treated very simply, as their delicate flavor is easily masked.

Tomato

More tomatoes are grown in California than anywhere else in the country, supplying the nation with 90% of its processed tomatoes and about 50% of its fresh tomatoes. Californians have a love/hate relationship with tomatoes. They love them so much they'll even buy the ones they hate. Those offered in the supermarket are rarely vine ripened. They are picked green, when they have enough tensile strength to survive processing and shipping, and allowed to ripen as best they can en route. And when that's all that's available the Golden Staters will buy them, and complain as they eat them. At the supermarket your best bet is cherry tomatoes. Because they can be packed in small, protective plastic boxes they can be picked fully ripe, or nearly so.

Tomatoes in all shapes, sizes, and colors

From June to November, though, the farmers' markets will provide an astounding variety of tomatoes, some of which don't even look like tomatoes. Fresh, ripe, slurpy, juicy, sweet, sunshiny tomatoes come in a dozen shades of red, some of them gold, others with zebra stripes or leopard spots. They come in all shapes and sizes. During the tomato season many of the better restaurants will offer a salad of mixed tomatoes. The dressing will be little more than a pinch of salt or a leaf of fresh basil. Anything more would be gilding the lily.

Tomatoes ready to burst with juicy flavor

HERBAL RENAISSANCE

Back when Simon and Garfunkel sang "parsley, sage, rosemary, and thyme," those were virtually the only herbs available. And parsley was more often next to the food, as garnish, than in it. We were living in the herbal dark ages.

Broadleaf parsley   *Variegated sage*   *Rosemary*   *Lemon thyme*

Then, in the early 1990s, arugula was introduced to Napa Valley chefs by specialty lettuce growers Peter Forni and Lynn Brown. Peppery and pungent, arugula soon transformed California's idea of what a salad could be. It may have been the beginning of an herbal renaissance. A few years later, when the Lazy Susan Ranch started growing and selling culinary herbs, my mission was to provide previously unavailable "exotic" herbs to professional chefs.

I had a list of favorites that I felt deserved a place in restaurant kitchens. Savory, for example. Complementary to familiar Mediterranean herbs like thyme and rosemary, there was nothing risqué about the mild, spicy flavor of savory. But at that time, chefs didn't use it. Also among my favorites was cucumber-flavored burnet, with its pretty, petite, scalloped leaves.

Arugula at the Marin County farmers' market

Purple basil

Tarragon

Angelica was another. A six-foot-tall plant with large hollow stems and elephant ear leaves, angelica has an unusual metallic flavor. Frequently candied in sugar syrup, angelica is used to perfume desserts. Or it can be stuffed, fresh from the earth, into the cavity of a large fish, and baked. I was a big promoter of shiso, also known as perilla, an herb whose ruffled purple and green leaves impart a distinctive flavor reminiscent of cumin.

In 1995, there was no demand for any of these. Traditional herbs like English thyme kept the farm afloat while I preached about my "exotics" with missionary zeal. None of these herbs is new. Most were forgotten as Americans emigrated from the "old country," east, west, or south, and are now being rediscovered by a generation of creative Californians.

Italian basil

Borage   *Oregano*   *Chives*

By 1999, chefs began to clamor for new flavors. Once word got out that there was a source for the likes of lemon verbena and lovage, restaurants began to experiment with them. Adventurous chefs who visited my gardens discovered unique oriental herbs like rau ram with its citrusy cilantro-like flavor, and kaffir lime leaves, traditionally used to perfume Thai soups. There are Mexican herbs, like crunchy verdulaga, also known as purslane, and the brilliantly colored red amaranth. There is wild chamomile, or pineapple weed, and sleepers like stinging nettle. Just a decade after the first arugula titillated our taste buds, many Californian farmers have expanded beyond traditional English thyme to offer lemon and lime thyme. Forni and Brown, who introduced arugula, now offer nepitella, whose flavor is a marriage of mint and marjoram.

The arugula salads of the 1990s seem tame today. However, arugula has now been upstaged by rucola, sometimes referred to as rustic or wild arugula, an herb with a similar but much more pungent radish flavor, for serious devotees only. In just a few years, herbs that were once considered exotic have become staples in Californian kitchens.

Today, my eight-acre herb farm can't keep up with the demand for herbs that no one even wanted 10 years ago. How lucky we are, with this unlimited palette of fresh flavors, to cook and eat in the midst of the herbal renaissance!

Linda-Marie Bauer, **W** *www.lazysusanranch.com*

Copper fennel

Fruits & Nuts

The USA is composed of 50 states, and in 49 of them California is sometimes called the "granola state," because it is said to be full of fruits and nuts. And, as with most other crops, California is the greatest producer all round. All but the most temperamental exotic tropical fruits are grown in California. And those are imported, year round, so you'll never be without. The orange is the fruit California is most closely associated with, and for a while, in the first half of the 20th century, that was good enough. In SoCal (Southern California) there is even a county called Orange. Its airport is named for movie star John Wayne, and it is the home of Disneyland.

California still produces huge quantities of oranges, but also huge quantities of so many other fruits: figs, cherries, watermelons, peaches of highest repute, apples in infinite variety, perfect pears, kiwi, cantaloupe and cassava. Even the prickly pear, the pad of a local cactus plant is grown here and makes a fine jam.

Freshly picked strawberries, Napa

Ripe watermelons

Nuts? You want nuts? They got nuts. All kinds of nuts. This state is the greatest producer of pistachios and walnuts. And it is the only commercial source of almonds in North America. You read that right. The almond growers of the Central Valley supply not only the domestic market, but also those of Europe, India, and China. Not content with mere mass production, they also regularly create new varieties. The latest, to our knowledge, is the Marchini, developed and patented by grower Joseph Marchini of Merced County. They're very crunchy and tasty, and go well with a dry martini. Go Joe!

English walnuts

Almonds

STAPLES

Meyer Lemon

Take a walk through the suburban neighborhoods of Oakland, Berkeley, or Richmond on the eastern shore of San Francisco Bay. On every second or third block you'll encounter a lemon tree whose fruit looks just a little bit odd and whose leaves emit a fragrance that seems too sweet to be lemon. It's almost a lemonade tree. It's actually the Meyer lemon. Most lemons in California are either the Eureka or the Lisbon variety. They have thick, glossy rinds that express much oil, their pulp is tightly packed, and the fruit is quite sour. Few people could eat a fresh whole lemon and enjoy it. But California's Meyer lemon is a "whole 'nother" fruit.

It's easy to spot a Meyer lemon. The skin is very obviously quite thin. It can have an almost shriveled appearance, and it lacks luster. And the ends are less tapered than the other varieties. So maybe it's the ugly duckling of lemons. But it's a swan underneath. It bursts with juice. And more importantly, it can be sweet enough to eat on its own. It is also cooked into savories and sweets – the whole fruit can be used, peel, pulp, pith, and all. Slices of the whole fruit are tossed into salads, or battered and deep-fried to be served alongside calamari or hot dogs. It makes a lovely lemonade, a super sorbet, and a great granita. The Meyer is now being grown commercially and is available in specialty shops, farmers' markets and the better class of supermarket throughout most of the year. The Charbay Company of California even produces a Meyer lemon vodka. As of now, though, most Meyer lemon trees are still grown on the lawns and in the backyards of suburban neighborhoods. Those that overhang the sidewalk are available to the pedestrian. If you meet any Berkeleyites, there is a good chance one of them has several such trees marked on a city map.

Avocado

In the front yard of a tidy little house on West Road in La Habra, California, grows what many have come to call the "Mother Tree." This sturdy and enduring tree is the first known of its breed, the Haas avocado. The area in which it still stands was formerly a vast acreage of avocado trees. Now it is a vast acreage of middle-class suburban homes. Yet while all the other trees have been ripped out, none would think of removing the Mother Tree, so dearly do Californians esteem the avocado. California and the avocado are almost synonymous.

The avocado is believed to have originated in southern Mexico. Several varieties of this rich and buttery fruit had made their way north to California during the mission period. By 1924 the Golden State was growing and exporting to the world 19 varieties of what was often called the "alligator pear." The most

Ripe Haas avocados

common variety was the one known as the Fuerte. But then came a postal worker from the town of Whittier (home to both M. F. K. Fisher and Richard Nixon) named Rudolph Haas. An avid gardener and part-time orchardist, Haas purchased a gross of avocado seedlings from a local nursery. All those that took root and flourished were fairly ordinary trees bearing fairly ordinary fruit. Except for one. Its fruit was unusually dark and the skin was covered with what looked like little warts. And its flesh was richer and more flavorful than any Haas had ever tasted. Since then the Haas avocado has been equal with the orange as the signature fruit of California. Today 85% of California's avocado crop is Haas.

The quintessential avocado recipe is for guacamole (whok-a-mo-lay). This dish is ancient. The Aztecs enjoyed it long before Cortez and the Conquistadores arrived to upset the table. Californians are hardly able to think of things like the margarita cocktail, corn chips, or sunshine, without thinking of guacamole.

Guacamole

Ingredients

2	large Haas avocados
½	onion, grated
2	fresh serrano or jalapeno chiles (with stems and seeds removed), finely minced
1	chopped tomato or the juice of 1 lime
2 tbs	chopped cilantro (coriander)
	salt to taste

Split the avocados and scoop their flesh into a bowl. Add all the other ingredients, and toss and mash the mix with a fork, or whisk, until a lumpy paste is achieved. Guacamole should never be smooth, but have chunks that offer something to the teeth.

Makes about 2½ cups (625mL)

STAPLES

Prawns with guacamole, Napa Valley wine auction, St Helena

Meat, Fish & Fowl

Californians are great lovers of flesh. Although vegetarians are greatly represented, red meat is almost the state dish. Golden Staters, however, are not overly given to complex recipes for beef, lamb, pork, or game. They like their meat meaty, red, full-flavored, and with just a bit of marbling. One of the most popular dishes here is carpaccio, thinly sliced raw beef laid out on a plate and dressed with olive oil, lemon, capers, grated parmesan cheese, and parsley. From time to time, trendy places will offer this dish made from ostrich breast, or ahi tuna. And they are very good, too.

Beef

California vies with Illinois, Kansas, and Texas for the best beef in the nation. For many years the paradigm for beef was corn-fed beef from the Midwest. It is richly marbled, full of protein and flavor, juicy, and tender. In California, however, a reverse trend is in progress. Many of the better restaurants are now serving "grass-fed" beef. This is from cattle left to range freely, feeding on the sweet local grasses, and growing fat and happy without the aid of dietary supplements. This is just as their pastoral predecessors did in times gone by. Their meat is not as tender as that of corn-fed cattle, but is much more flavorful. It also has a texture that most people prefer, often called "chewy" or "al dente". Should you see "grass-fed" on the menu, we recommend you consider it.

Where's the beef? In California!

Grass-fed or no, when it comes to beef, Californians have their favorites. One of the old standbys is known as the London broil. Our apologies to the residents of London, for we know that this does not exist in their fair city. The London broil is not a single cut of meat, but a thick selection of skirt, or flank. A large slab of beef, sometimes nearly a foot long and 9 inches wide, is usually marinated, and cooked over coals or under the broiler. Before serving it is sliced, very thinly, crosswise against the grain. It is a staple of backyard barbecues, camp cooks, and people who don't know what else to do with themselves at dinnertime.

Prime rib is a cut of meat by no means unique to California. Midwesterners pride themselves on the quality of theirs. And they are not without cause. Texans just assume that theirs is the best, even though they might not actually know what it is. California simply serves it forth. This is a slice of rare roasted beef taken from the standing rib, sans bone. A typical roast will hold anywhere from three to seven wide, meaty ribs. It is generally roasted quite plain, though it may be honored with a spice rub in California. It is much more tender than a steak, and more juicy. It is also thicker, being at least as thick as a beef rib, which is darned thick! In the Golden State a prime rib is pretty much taken for granted in traditional restaurants. Your leading-edge joints won't have it. Alice's restaurant (Chez Panisse) won't have it. But the roadhouse will, the steak house will, and so will many Italian places.

So you want a steak, with no complications, and no questions asked beyond, "rare, medium, or well done?" These days the flatiron steak is all the rage, and will be for some time. It's delicious, juicy, and low in fat. It is cut from the shoulder, and looks a bit like a flank steak. It is usually served with potato or rice, and a vegetable side dish. You know, typical steak house fare. A popular menu item these days is "steak frites." This is a steak, quickly grilled, served with french fries. Usually nothing else accompanies this dish unless you ask for it.

Chile Con Carne

It's true, chile con carne (usually just referred to as "chile") did not originate in California. But this is nothing strange. Very little actually originates in California, other than trends and ideas. It's what California does with things that makes the difference.

We know that though chile relies on the chief crops of Mexico, it did

> ### Chillin'
> The term "chile con carne" is Spanish for "chile with meat," and refers to meat cooked with hot chile pepper (*Capsicum frutescens*). Although it is sometimes spelled "chilli" or "chili," we use the pungent pod's locally preferred Spanish/Mexican spelling – "chile" – in this book.

not come from Mexico. Earliest written references are from the Lone Star State, Texas, and date from the mid-19th century. Here we find a custom of pounding together dried beef, suet, salt, and crushed red chile pepper. The resulting mass was then molded and pressed into the shape of a brick and would keep for months. It could be used by homesteaders in winter, cowboys on the cattle drive, or gold seekers to California as a savory addition to beans or other vegetable foods, or could even be eaten plain and uncooked while on the march. These "chile bricks" were often referred to as "American pemmican," a comparison to the concentrated dried meat staple consumed by plains Indians at the time.

Later in the same century it evolved into the chopped or ground meat stew, often with red beans and tomatoes, with which we are familiar today. Virtually every region in the USA and parts of Canada has its version.

Serrano pepper

Death Wish

"Wish I had time for just one more bowl of chile."

Western frontiersman Kit Carson's last words

Texas still holds fairly close to the original, usually without the beans or tomatoes. In Ohio they are known to make it with Middle Eastern spices and serve it over pasta. The whole country serves chile dogs – a hot dog in a bun with chile poured over it. They're impossible to eat without making a mess. And they're delicious, too. You'll also find chile burgers, chile fries, chile rice, chile eggs, and even chile pie.

What distinguishes California chile from its cousins? It is generally a more complex recipe, relying on layers of flavor more than on the heat of the dominant spice. It usually includes beans, with kidney beans the most common. Sometimes the finished dish is called "chile beans." And it is usually dressed for the fair, in comparison to its more dowdy kin. Customary garnishes are offered, such as chopped onion, grated cheese, avocado, oyster crackers or corn chips, sour cream, salsa, ketchup, even fruit compote. In San Francisco you may order buffalo chile at Tommy's Joint, where the dish has been on offer for over 100 years.

For all its countrywide variations, the chile in California is the most famous. And that is due in large part to Dave Chasen of the now-closed Chasen's restaurant in Hollywood. It was situated at the corner of Doheny and Beverly Boulevards, near Melrose Avenue and Santa Monica Boulevard. It was a plush, wood-paneled, leather-boothed Hollywood eatery where many uproarious goings-on went on. Its best-known and most-loved menu item was its chile con carne. Flocks of film stars came to drink fine booze at the horseshoe bar and eat Chasen's chile, on site or to take away. Eleanor Roosevelt (wife of Franklin D.) asked for the recipe and was politely denied, but sent a complementary quart. J. Edgar Hoover, director of the FBI, proclaimed it the best chile in the world. Humphrey Bogart and Jack Benny ate it regularly. And to give it the equivalent of a papal blessing, Elizabeth Taylor had it shipped to her, on dry ice, when she was in Italy shooting the motion picture Cleopatra with Richard Burton. The record does not reveal whether her paramour enjoyed it as well. It's also generally believed that Chasen's chile is to have provided Clark Gable with his last meal before he died of lung cancer. The building formerly occupied by Chasen's now houses a branch of Bristol Farms Market, an upscale supermarket of good repute. One corner of the building is preserved as a little bit of Chasen's, complete with its original wood paneling and leather booths. And, of course, the famous chile con carne. When in Hollywood, go for Gable's getaway grub. Look for it on our map (p152).

Other Meats & Meat Products
Lamb

The range wars of the western frontier produced a lot of bad blood between cattlemen and sheep herders, and resentments can still be detected today. Throughout the Southwest there are people who continue to disdain lamb. But they don't live in the Golden State.

In the home kitchen you'll most commonly find lamb as simple chops or a roasted leg. The chops will be done simply, while a leg might be simple or quite elaborate. Most restaurants serve it as "rack of lamb." Ribs can be cooked plainly, or can be rubbed with herbs and basted with wine. California has a number of Moroccan restaurants where it is served baked with honey and almonds, whereas home cooks are fond of garlic and rosemary.

Skewers of lamb and vegetables, Faz Restaurant, Marriott Courtyard Hotel, San Diego

Pork

The heavenly pig (with apologies to our Jewish and Muslim friends) has had a bad rap in recent years due to its fat content. There has been a movement among some advertisers, politically correct dietitians, and people with no useful labor to perform, to denounce pork as being bad for the health. It is noteworthy to note that these same folk say little or nothing about the importance of exercise, a balanced diet, exercise, moderation, and, most importantly, exercise. If you should shop for pork at the market, we recommend that you look for rich marbling, and if you don't see it, buy something else. At a restaurant your best bet is usually a smoked chop. If you want true pork satisfaction, you are perfectly within your rights to see the uncooked portion prior to ordering. And don't forget the importance of exercise.

Lolas Mexican meat market in Santa Rosa

Sausage

There was a time when sausage was almost always pork, very fatty, sometimes smoked. Stroll through a high-end market these days and you'll find it made from anything. Turkey is common, as it is low in fat. Duck sausage is superb (they can't get all the fat out). Lamb, chicken, and rabbit all find their way into sausage, as do shellfish such as scallops. Sometimes the sausage is smoked, sometimes spiced, and sometimes just plain if the meat is flavorsome. And of course you can still get that delicious fatty pork sausage. Sausage in California is mainly home food, where pork sausages are common for breakfast; Polish sausage sandwiches make a good lunch; and grilled Italian or Cajun sausages are often served for dinner. A high-end bar & grill may also offer sausages, as might a Basque or Italian place.

Fish

With some 1,000 miles of coastline, innumerable miles of rivers and streams, and scores of lakes, it can be no wonder that Californians are mad for finny fare whether from salt water or sweet. Fishing is not only a huge industry, but also one of the most popular outdoor sports. Virtually everyone who doesn't go fishing knows somebody who does. And those who do not fish with hook and line do so with spears, and if not that then they go picking about the tidepools at low tide for mussels, cockles, and limpets, or diving off the shore to collect abalone. They will stand on the shore in the midst of the surf with triangular nets to scoop up shoals of smelt. And then there are those intrepid souls who go hunting for shark.

Californians love their finny fare

Salmon

Captains Lewis and Clark were commissioned by President Thomas Jefferson to explore and chart a huge tract of land known as the Louisiana Purchase, which stretched from the Mississippi River to the Pacific Ocean. Their first gastronomic encounter with the Pacific region was with smoked salmon

Salmon as art

given to them by the Indians. Salmon is a great culinary constant of the entire Pacific coast. Local economies and cultures are sustained and informed by it. The indigenous tribes still celebrate the annual return of the salmon with a ceremony called "First Fish." Many local fishermen observe the custom of kissing and then releasing the first salmon they catch, as a gesture of thanks and for good luck.

Whole communities experience a kind of "salmon fever" of excitement when the fish are running. As with the wines of California, harvesting and enjoying the salmon is a gustatory experience born of the natural bounty, culture, and traditions of its region. You will have no trouble finding it when you go to the Golden State.

Just-caught salmon, Fort Bragg

Chilean Sea Bass

According to the United States Food and Drug Administration, this critter is a Patagonian toothfish. "And our special tonight, sir, is a filet of Patagonian toothfish." How many people would order that? With the more appetizing name of Chilean sea bass, this fish shot to popularity around 10 years ago. Since then, Californians have been mad for it and have embraced it as their own.

The Chilean sea bass is actually a member of the cod family, closely related to the Northern Pacific sablefish, or black cod. It is found in the higher latitudes of the southern hemisphere, in deeper, colder waters. Fish in such environments are commonly high in fat, necessary for survival as a kind of organic antifreeze. The toothfish is fattier than most salmon, and so is ideal for dry cooking techniques such as barbecuing or broiling.

However, its popularity has led to overfishing, mainly by pirate fishing fleets. Because it takes around eight years to reach sexual maturity, this fish is especially vulnerable to overfishing. According to the National Environmental Trust in Washington, unless pressure on the species is decreased, the Chilean sea bass could become commercially extinct within five years. Heeding their warning, many restaurateurs in California, and throughout the US, have taken the fish off their menus in a bid to save the species. For more information visit the National Environmental Trust's website at W www.environet.policy.net/marine/csb.

Pacific Halibut

This tasty beastie is found all along the Pacific coast, from the Bering Sea to central California. It's a standard of the fish house and a frequent special in other restaurants when in season. As a bottom dweller it can't be taken by net, so commercial fishers take them by longline. Halibut is also a favorite game fish, especially with divers. It's available fresh from March to November, and frozen the year round. The meat is relatively lean, so dry cooking is not favored. However, it is excellent for braising, frying, poaching, and baking. The flesh is firm and white, flakes easily and is succulent when skillfully prepared. It has a milder taste than many other fish, so if you like your fish not so fishy, halibut might be for you.

STAPLES

GHOSTLY FARE?

One of the enduring legacies of the Gold Rush is an abundance of ghost towns. Wherever a gold (or later, silver) strike occurred, small cities sprang up overnight. A typical town would have some fine houses and a lot of shacks, a handful of general stores and outfitters, an indeterminate number of brothels, 40 saloons, and a church. Many even had daily newspapers and their correspondents included the likes of Mark Twain and Bret Harte.

While the works of those scribes are still alive, most of the towns are not. When the gold or silver ran out, so did the populace. As quickly as the towns had sprung to life, so did they die. Folks just packed up their portable goods and left without closing the door. Some towns were eventually burnt to the ground by spontaneous combustion, lightning strikes, or wanton vandalism. Others, shoddily built in haste, quickly decayed and sank back into the earth. Yet others have stood up remarkably well. And the generations that came after the 49ers (see p12) began to cherish them as time capsules, as monuments to that magnificent, feverish adventure known as the Gold Rush. Surviving ghost towns were acquired by the state government and have been designated as historic parks. There is one ghost town, known today as China Camp, that is unique in two ways: its reason for being did not relate to something valuable being buried deep in the ground; and not all its residents are ghosts.

Forty-niners came from all over the globe, including China – mostly from the southern province of Guangdong (Canton). In Cantonese dialect the name California is rendered as "Gold Mountain." It was the average Chinese 49er's plan to do what most other 49ers had in mind: strike it rich and go back home, perhaps to lord it over the neighbors. Some had more modest plans, to make only a certain sum that would allow them to return home and buy a farm or other enterprise. But fate had other things in mind for the adventurers, regardless of whence they came.

Shellfish
Oysters

Oysters are almost synonymous with the California shoreline, and have been since the Gold Rush. Fried oysters are fine, and so are oyster stew, oyster omelet, and oyster loaf. But Californian connoisseurs like them best raw, naked right from the shell. In days gone by the oyster bar was commonplace – this was an establishment dedicated to oysterology and little else. Those places are now few, but oysters are not. They have simply

Most went broke. And most never went home, for many reasons. Perhaps home held no opportunity. Some were wanted by the law, by wives, or by creditors. In China political instability was rife and it was near impossible to make a decent living. And then there was California, and the 49ers had discovered that she had many kinds of gold.

Canton is the site of one of the principal shrimp fisheries of China, and many of the Chinese gold seekers had been shrimpers. They quickly learned that San Francisco Bay teemed with what are called "grass shrimp," so-called because after hatching in the open Bay waters they migrate to a protective salt grass where they grow to adulthood. The men of Canton-and-California built boats and made nets after their tradition, and for decades the waters of the Golden Gate bore the junks and sampans of the East alongside the clipper ships and schooners of the West.

This marine gold rush outlasted the terrestrial by decades. But it did not last forever. Overfishing had its inevitable effect on the shrimp population. The runoff from High Sierra hydraulic mining that affected the oyster beds also began to choke off the salt grass. Human population growth and shoreline housing development began to squeeze out the shrimping villages. By the 1920s only a few remained, and their catch was no longer sustaining them.

But there was one stubborn holdout – China Camp. It struggled gamely into the mid-20th century, but lost inhabitants year by year. The state then acquired the little ghost town on the shore of Marin County, and in 1977 opened it as a historic park. Despite its status as a public park, and ghost town, it is still occupied by the Quan family. They operate the village general store, established by one of their ancestors. Mr. Quan rents boats to visitors, and he still takes his own out in search of the grass shrimp. These days his catch is so low that he generally sells it for bait. But on certain lucky days he will bring in enough that his wife, Georgette, can sell shrimp cocktails to visitors. All who taste them say that they are the sweetest shrimp in the world. Maybe that's because they are tasting history.

moved on to other venues. Nowadays many restaurants incorporate what is known as the "raw bar." It offers oysters, as well as sushi, raw scallops, tuna carpaccio, mussels, and yet more oysters. Large oysters are taken directly from the shell. Smaller ones are often served as an "oyster shooter." This is a shucked, small oyster dropped into a bartender's shot glass and dressed with a tomato-based cocktail sauce, with maybe a bit of horseradish, and even a drop of tequila. You knock it back neat just like a drink. But don't forget to chew.

STAPLES

Oyster

n. A slimy, gobby shellfish which civilization gives men the hardihood to eat without removing its entrails! The shells are sometimes given to the poor.

Ambrose Bierce,
The Devil's Dictionary, 1911

Organized and sustained commercial exploitation of the oyster fishery began in the 1850s. Gold seekers and other immigrants had an enormous appetite for oysters. Every waterfront saloon offered them, every hotel dining room, every restaurant of any repute (and many with none) offered oysters. Californians were ape for oysters. The state has imported, developed, and farmed numerous varieties, but perhaps the most popular nowadays is the Kumamoto, a variety of the Pacific. It's larger, with a deeper cup that makes for more satisfying slurping.

Supplying Californians with enough oysters has long been a challenge, but perhaps the most colorful problem to overcome was the rise in the late 19th century of the "oyster pirates." Oysters were as valuable as the far-flung spices of old or the narcotics of today. When such money and adventure is to be had, even moral men are tempted to set their consciences aside to ride the whirlwind and reap the bounty. The oyster beds so painstakingly cared for by the early aquaculturists were plundered nightly by men in small, fast sloops. The state government had to hire special oyster sheriffs to bring the bad men to heel.

Collecting oysters

THE WALRUS AND THE CARPENTER

"O Oysters," said the carpenter,
"You've had a pleasant run!
Shall we be trotting home again?"
But answer came there none –
And this was scarcely odd, because
They'd eaten every one.

Lewis Carroll

Despite the preponderance of the Kumamoto oyster, there is good variety to be had in California. An oyster tasting is a popular opening to a fine dinner on the town. A dozen oysters, with two each of six different varieties, is the norm for a party of two. It's not uncommon to follow with another dozen of the two varieties they find most tasty. And what they find most tasty will change over time and season. The taste and texture of an oyster is highly dependent on its food and the temperature and salinity of its environment. These are always in flux.

Abalone

The abalone has a mystique that in some ways surpasses the oyster's. Perhaps this is because most Californians have never tasted it and never will. At one time it was common, and considered food for the poor. Oyster snobs would shun it. By comparison with the oyster the abalone was thought of as a humble mollusk whose flesh was as tough as a boot, which had to be pounded not into tenderness but into submission, and was not worth the effort. "Let it be food for Indians and failed miners," was the attitude. But by the 19th century the attitude was changing.

Of the genus *Haliotis*, meaning "ear shaped," it looks somewhat like a clam on the half-shell. In fact it is a marine snail, but with its hemispherical shell it appears nothing like its terrestrial cousin, the escargot. It can make a ceviche if sliced thinly enough and soaked in lime juice. But the only universally acceptable way to serve abalone is breaded and flash-fried. The best cooks will dredge it in flour, dip it in egg wash, then pat it with finely crushed soda crackers. It is then shallow-fried for 30 seconds per side in olive oil or clarified butter. Adding any kind of sauce is considered to be going over the top, although a squeeze of lemon and a few capers are permitted by all but the most ardent purists. In Baja California, down Mexico way, we have seen it dressed with a creamy crab sauce.

Very few restaurants offer this treat that sells at retail for as much as $35 per pound. Only caviar sells for more, and one is not expected to make a meal of that. Sigh. A nascent abalone farming industry supplies specialty shops, and you can find them with a simple Web search. The greatest number of abalone taken today is by sport divers who enjoy it at home and reward their friends with it. If you are a diver, bring your gear, or rent some at Monterey, Santa Barbara, or Fort Bragg. In the south there are no abalone available near the shore, so all are taken in deep water using air tanks. In the north it's the reverse, tanks are not allowed. Abalone must be taken by free diving from the shore where they tend to cluster. Again, a simple Web search will put you in touch with ab diving clubs. An alternative, if you are in the south, is to take a side trip to Tijuana or Ensenada, Mexico. Abs are still more plentiful there. The Cueva de los Tigres restaurant in Ensenada claims to serve more abalone than any restaurant in the world. A lot of it with creamy crab sauce.

Fowl

So you want birds? In California, choose your feather and the flock is yours. Chicken, duck, goose, partridge, grouse, ptarmigan, or quail can all grace your table. There are a few restaurants that specialize in game and game birds; however, most restaurants use what fowl is generally available. And some offer what are known as free-range birds, or liberty birds. Free-range fowl are domestic birds that are allowed to roam quite freely. Liberty fowl have less freedom of movement, but are not confined to pens. In either case, the little birdies can strut about, pecking at delicious things on the ground, enjoying their days, preening themselves, and generally becoming tasty and tender.

Chicken

In the restaurant and at the market the most common bird is the chicken. There are many on sale that are trucked in from other regions. But if you've come to California, why bother with them? Golden State birds are better. This is not merely opinion, but an immutable law of nature. At the market, ask for free-range birds.

Duck

When out to eat in California, the specialty fowl is duck. In a Chinese eatery it might be roasted to a chestnut brown in the imperial style, or barbecued with a vivid red color. In a California-style restaurant you may enjoy a melt-in-your-mouth confit of duck leg, a pan-seared breast served rare on a bed of aromatic brown or basmati rice, or even a velvety-smooth duck-liver flan. In 1875, the first commercial duck farm in California was located in what is now the Mission district of San Francisco. The variety raised at that farm was the Pekin, brought to the USA from China by a clipper ship captain who had acquired a taste for them in Shanghai. The Pekin is still the most common variety in California. You may also see the Muscovy duck, a leaner bird with a wild game taste that many prefer. And there is the Moulard, a hybrid of the two, raised mainly for foie gras. The most famous duck is from the town of Petaluma in California. The descendants of that same San Francisco duck farmer of 1875 are the state's provider of Petaluma duck.

Turkey

Turkey, everlasting turkey, will flood the market at Thanksgiving (late November) and at Christmas. But otherwise you will not see much of this noble fowl. This is a pity, as a roast of turkey is a fine dinner. But you can always place a special order with the butcher. Some restaurants will also accommodate you if you give them enough notice.

> ### Turkey
>
> n. A large bird whose flesh when eaten on certain religious anniversaries has the peculiar property of attesting piety and gratitude. Incidentally, it is pretty good eating.
>
> *Ambrose Bierce,*
> The Devil's Dictionary, *1911*

STAPLES

Turkey legs on the barbecue

STAPLES

Cheese

"Processed cheese" is perhaps the most common form of cheese across the USA. This is simple, cheddar-like stuff that has been bulked up and made bland and consistent by doses of supplements such as whey solids and food coloring. You can get it anywhere. But California is the best place in America for cheese because its chefs, homemakers, and restaurant-goers demand that it be so. The beautiful state of Wisconsin is known as "the dairy state," and this moniker is even a part of its automobile number plate. By official count, Wisconsin produces more cheese than any other state in the union, with California running second. However, should it come to light how much cheese and processed cheese Wisconsin imports from California to make its own products, the standings might be reversed. Be that as it may, we think very highly of the California product, especially its artisanal cheeses, the variety of which seems infinite.

Artisanal cheeses are made by hand, and paddle

It is fitting, though, that this natural partner to wine should be so abundant in the center of North American wine culture. There are around 130 types of cheese produced by more than 50 large and small producers. All the cheeses with which you are familiar, both locally made and imported, are here. And the artisanal products – those made in small batches by hand using traditional methods – are constantly changing. They change with the seasons because the feed consumed by the cows, nanny goats, and ewes changes with the seasons, and so does their milk. They change because their artisans are always experimenting. They will alter the milk blend, stud the cheese with bits of hot pepper, dot it with herbs, or dose it with mold or even ash. At the famous Cowgirl Creamery in Marin County, they wrap a soft-ripening cheese in local stinging nettles. Don't worry,

Four-footed Californian ready to make cheese, Redwood Hill Farm, Sebastopol

the nettles have been unstung, yet they lend a spicy zing to the mild cheese. You can watch the cheese being made at the Cowgirl, which is located in a restored hay barn at Point Reyes Station on the Marin coast. The shop, which sells the cheese as well as bread and lots of picnic food, is separated from the cheesery by a glass partition, so you are able to drool at the cheese-making process from a distance.

Brie is just one of California's many cheeses. Perhaps the most famous brand of this soft-ripening cheese is Rouge et Noir, in production for over 100 years. From the Central Valley comes teleme (tel-a-mee), a buttery, mild cheese wrapped in rice paper. Smoked cheeses are common, as are goat's milk cheeses such as chèvre. Camellia (a camembert-style cheese), carmody (a semifirm cheese with a buttery flavor), crescenza (a rich, creamy cheese), and camembert might all appear on the cheese board in better restaurants. The house cheesemaster will advise you in which order to take them.

California's most famous cheese, its own indigenous cheese, is known as Monterey Jack. It is a white, cheddar-like cheese when fresh. When aged and dried it closely resembles parmesan cheese. It is often dosed with chile pepper and then is known as pepper Jack. There is some misunderstanding as to its origin and name. Contrary to legend, there was no cheesemaker called Monterey Jack. There was a certain David Jacks who lived in

Goat cheese, Redwood Hill Farm, Sebastopol

An assortment of cheeses, Dean & DeLuca, St Helena

Monterey and shipped cheeses from there. But this cheese had been made in Monterey long before he was around. Its recipe goes back to the days of Spanish California, when it was known as *queso del pais*, or country cheese. It was made with a vicelike contraption that pressed the curds into a compact shape. In English this press was known as a housejack. Hence, cheese from the jack in Monterey came to be known as Monterey Jack. Its taste is mild to medium. It also melts well and so makes an excellent fondue.

Bread

Even before the culinary "cultural revolution" of the 1970s (see p16), California was well known for its bread, at least in San Francisco. The local sourdough has been famous since Gold Rush days. It has been sold at San Francisco International Airport for as long as anyone can remember, so that folks can take it home to other parts of the country. That's because they can't make it in other parts of the country. Sourdough, wherever it comes from, depends on the local wild yeast and a little bug called Lactobacillus. The wild yeast makes the bread rise, and the Lactobacillus releases its own local style of lactic acid, thus giving the bread its distinctive sour taste. The species *Lactobacillus sanfrancisco* cannot live outside its own little niche in a corner of the city of Saint Francis. So if you want more than a traveler's taste of this bread, you've got to come and get it.

Bread with a twist

But in other parts of the state the bread story was traditionally that of the rest of the country. People once ate bland, thinly sliced, aerated stuff, stripped of many of its nutrients and called fortified or enriched. It was good enough for kids' sandwiches, or to receive slathers of peanut butter and jam. But you wouldn't want to boast about the stuff. Then came the revolution. Many people credit Steve Sullivan, early of Chez Panisse, with starting the bread culture that is now an integral part of Californian life. In the early 1980s he started Acme bakery, where he produced rich, full-flavored, heavily textured breads in the European/Mediterranean style. These are big, golden, thickly crusted, and aromatic creatures of the bread kingdom. They shout nutrition, they speak taste, they sing satisfaction, and promise nourishment of both body and soul. The operation at Acme instantly sparked a legion of worthy imitators. Now, up and down the state, loaves of pain levain, baguettes, rounds of both sourdough and sweet breads, seed-crusted rolls, and rye, wheat, and barley breads are found daily at the bakeries and better supermarkets.

Artisan bakers grind their own flour

Faces of Gastronomy – THE VILLAGE BAKER

In an old neighborhood in the deep south Californian town of Escondido, on the old road to Palm Springs, sits what looks like a neat little house. The local pedestrians are a colorful, eclectic mix of high and low, left and right. And they all sniff the air as they pass by. Some stop, look, and follow the aroma into the little "house," which in fact is the artisanal bakery of Mr. Frederick Holmshaw. When we followed the aroma we found Fred grinding his own flour for one of the two dozen different breads he produces, by hand, every working day.

Atrisanal bakery, Escondido

"Well, I wasn't to the manor born," he says when we ask how he came to this line of work. "I started out with an MBA and a career as a marketing executive. But the endless pursuit of profit just never really satisfied me. Besides, I like to be able to do things my own way. And having spent some time in France I was able to learn to appreciate good food and good bread, and to slow down enough to enjoy it."

Weighing the dough   *Preparing for baking*

His own way is with the most serious attention to quality ingredients, and to the traditional methods of the old time "village bakery." He explains how before the industrial revolution everything was done by hand, by skilled workers, artisans. With the coming of industry artisans found themselves displaced, and had to go to work in factories. "And the close personal relationship between worker and product, the human element, was lost. So I'm part of a 'movement' of sorts to restore the village bakery. There are a few dozen of us artisanal bakers here in California, and our numbers are growing. We don't use conditioners or artificial ingredients, we don't mass produce. So I'll never get rich at this. But hey, I guess I'm just a romantic."

Into the oven   *Voilà! Ready to eat.*

Olives & Oil

Californians use more olive oil than any other collection of Yankees. And have done so for longer than any other Yankees. Olive trees have been grown here since Spanish days, and the first written record of their planting is dated 1769. But the general use of olive oil is relatively recent. Even today most of it is imported from Italy, with smaller amounts from Greece, Spain, Turkey, and France. The original plantings were rather small, and since then most olives grown in California, harvested black and ripe, have been for table use rather than for oil. Unfortunately, they are tinned and rather lacking in flavor.

Californian oil just keeps getting better

Young olives, McEvoy Ranch, Petaluma

The best Californian olives are among the best anywhere, but most are quite forgettable. This situation is mainly due to economics. Olive trees for oil require many years before they can bear, so the land brings no profit till then. When they do bear, they don't bring the same return as many other crops. A small number of growers with a great passion for olive oil (and a great purse) have been working to turn this situation around, with stunning results. In recent years Californian olive oil has been winning blind tastings in Europe, and blind loyalty at home. Check the farmers' markets and specialty shops. It's worth the effort.

California mission olives, "the old standbys of long standing"

Sweets

Californians tend to eat fewer sugary sweets than their compatriots. Living as they do in the fruit basket of the nation, they enjoy the natural goodies of the state. However, don't try to separate them from their gourmet ice cream – ice cream in any flavor you can imagine, and some you can't. Two popular brands include Ben & Jerry, and Bud's. The hot fudge sundae was popularized at drugstore counters, where ice-cream concoctions used to be sold. This is a dish of vanilla ice cream covered in rich, gooey hot chocolate fudge sauce, and topped with whipped cream and a maraschino cherry. Legend has it that film star Lana Turner was discovered while eating one at the counter of Schwabb's drugstore in Hollywood. Another popular Californian ice-cream treat is called the It's It. This is a slab of vanilla ice cream sandwiched between two large oatmeal cookies.

Burger, fries & a hot fudge sundae at Johnny Rockets, Los Angeles

Yogurt is commonplace, but Californians generally don't take it plain. They like it fruit-flavored. Most of it is made from cow's milk and contains gelatin to maintain consistency.

The good old-fashioned American milk shake is alive, though not always well. We think it is best had in dedicated ice-cream parlors, or in small countertop concerns where it is made with scoops of real ice cream and splashes of whole milk. In the Palm Springs area, where dates are cultivated, they use them to flavor milk shakes.

Yogurt cones   *Cotton candy, Santa Rosa farmers' market*

Then there's chocolate. The most famous here is by the Ghirardelli company of San Francisco. It began in the Gold Rush days, and developed the process by which cocoa butter could be separated from the dry cocoa powder using a filter system rather than the expensive hydraulic presses of the day. You can see displays of this at Ghirardelli Square. Former president Ronald Reagan's favorite sweetie was, and perhaps still is, jelly beans, made by the Jelly Belly company. You can find these wherever fine jelly beans are sold. Dedicated candy stores are not very common, with most people buying candies at the supermarket. For jelly beans, chocolate drops, gummy bears, and other small candies that are scoopable, the markets usually offer them in bulk, where you can scoop from a tub full of the stuff. It's much cheaper that way.

Candy from the Mendocino Chocolate Company

Young girl with her snow cone

Perhaps California's chief contribution to the world of sweets is the fortune cookie – although it originated in San Francisco's Japantown, it has become synonymous with Chinese restaurants. This is a simple, thin wafer cookie that is still quite soft when freshly cooked and warm. A strip of paper with an incantation or a prophesy is dropped onto it, and the still-soft cookie is folded over to enclose the fortune. As the cookie cools, it becomes crisp and hard. You can get the cookies custom-made in different flavors and colors, and with personalized messages.

drinks of california

The Golden State is best known for its wine, and justifiably so. But this is also one of the great beer-brewing centers of the Earth, the birthplace of famous cocktails, the best place in the Western world for fruit juice, and the capital of coffee culture. It's even known as the Republic of Tea.

Wine
History

There are two wine industries in California's history: the one before Prohibition and the one that came after. "What's Prohibition?" you ask. Well, from 1920 to 1933 a certain madness afflicted the great American people. They seduced themselves into thinking they could cure society's worser ills by banning demon rum, Mr. Booze, the evil influence of drink. They therefore passed a constitutional amendment banning alcohol from public life. However, in doing so they gave aid and comfort to the crime syndicates of the day, who until that time had eked out an uncertain living through gambling and stealing. But suddenly they had a huge market to serve, for the pious Americans would drink no less than before. The jazz age was lubricated with bootleg booze and sacramental wine.

BOOTLEGGER

During the Prohibition era many men were employed to smuggle illicit alcohol in quantities large and small. They employed all the types of ingenious ruses that modern drug smugglers use, with one addition – for a one- or two-bottle delivery they would simply slip a bottle into each of their high-topped, cowboy-style boots.

Let's ride to the saloon

Bodegas Santo Tomas winery paintings, Ensenada, Mexico

The first Californian wine industry began with the Spanish missionaries. It is believed that the first plantings were at Mission San Juan Capistrano in 1779. The grape was what is known as the "mission," and is still grown in California today, though in modest amounts. Its wine is not very remarkable, but then the missionaries were growing it for sacramental use, not for a fancy table. However, the frolicsome friars eventually made brandy with it, which was certainly not done by divine command. There is some debate on the origin of the mission grape, but DNA analysis has shown it to be of the species *Vitis vinifera*, indigenous to Europe. (Grapes indigenous to the Americas are not suitable for table wine.) It is thought to have originated in Spain as the criolla grape, and to have been carried to Baja California in the seabags of Spanish sailors from Peru, in the form of raisins. We know from his diary that Father Junipero Serra, the originator of the Californian mission chain (see p11), carried raisins with him during his trek from Baja to Alta California.

The Californios who followed in the wake of the missionaries soon became tired of drinking leftover altar wine, and by the 1830s premium varietals were being imported into California. Plantings increased markedly up and down the then Mexican province. Few folk had much viticultural knowledge at the time, so winemaking was a rather hit-and-miss proposition. But eventually certain areas were found to produce winning wines while others were better suited to, well, raisins. By the time those ragtag adventurers in Sonoma had their famous booze-up in 1846 (see p12), the Napa and Sonoma Valleys were recognized by some as world-class wine-growing regions.

When California became a US territory, and with the soon-to-follow Gold Rush, the market for its wines surged. And even the venerable General Vallejo got in on the act. After his ignoble seizure and many days of captivity in the "heady" days of 1846, he was treated honorably. He served in the senate of the new American state of California; one of his sons became the first native-born Californian to be commissioned as a US naval officer; an important town was named for him, and another for his wife, Benicia; his daughters had many beaus; and he grew wine. His label was known as Lacrima Montis (Tears of the Mountain). To this day there is a Sonoma winery that bears the general's name: M. G. Vallejo.

TAKE A BOW

Aah, here comes the wine, with great show and pomp. Perhaps, rather than the waiter, a real, live sommelier is serving it. He presents the bottle to our guest, who looks at it knowingly, and nods sagely. The sommelier pulls the cork, and discreetly sniffs it, then offers it for our guest's inspection. He or she eyes it, prods it, and approves. The wine-wise server pours a splash into the glass. Our excellent guest swirls, sniffs, takes a tentative sip, and comments on its balance and bouquet. After a moment's reflection, he proclaims it to his liking and authorizes it served. We have once again survived the solemn ceremony.

In all that theatrical trifling that goes with the serving of wine, only two things matter:

- That you witness the bottle being opened in your presence, after you have approved the label. This ensures you get what you pay for. If the wine isn't opened in front of you, send it back.
- That you will not need to sniff the cork, and that the wine will not require an enological analysis. The main purpose of the little ceremony is simply to determine whether the wine has spoiled in transit or storage (nowadays, spoilage is exceedingly rare).

With fits and starts, successes and failures, California's vintners sallied forth into the world and did their best to conquer. They did pretty well for a gang that did not have 3,000 years of custom, tradition, and handed-down knowledge of this arcane art, as their contemporaries in Europe did. In the late 19th century they actually won gold medals at Paris expositions. They made technological advances and scientific discoveries. They had among them flamboyant characters, such as "Count" Harazthy of Hungary. He is said to have introduced the zinfandel grape to California. He married two of his sons to General Vallejo's twin daughters. And, in an act suitable for a romantic novel by Garcia Ordoñez de Montalvo, he was eaten by a crocodile during a trip to Central America.

Thus it went, two steps forward and one step back, till that dark day when the Ladies' Christian Temperance Society and their ilk had their way, and Prohibition was enforced. Vineyards did not disappear, as most supplied grapes for the table. Most wineries closed, but not all, including the Napa Valley's Beaulieu winery, for there was a provision in the new law that allowed for the commercial production of sacramental wine. Because of this, Beaulieu was well positioned when the hateful law was repealed. Martini and Bundschu were likewise blessed with church contracts to supply the altars of those good citizens who would leave church after Mass to find the bootlegger.

There was also a number of independent operators that were supplying the sacramental wine market. While at that time it was easy to pick a Catholic priest (who was therefore authorized to buy or make wine for holy use), anyone could look like a Jewish rabbi. Rabbis were also authorized to purchase wine, and it was astonishing to note the increase in the population of rabbis – it is thought that at one time in the late 1920s the number of rabbis in California exceeded the number of Jews.

Mission chapel in Sonoma

I am usually very calm over the displays of Nature, but you will scarce believe how my heart leaped at this. It was like meeting one's wife. I had come home again.

Robert Louis Stevenson, upon taking up residence in the Californian wine country, 1879

WINE TO GO

There was a time in the state of California when restaurants only sold premium wine by the bottle. In a saloon or a roadhouse you might have bought a glass of jug wine at the bar, but to imbibe wine by the glass at your table was virtually unheard of. If you did purchase a bottle at your table, you were well advised to drink it all, because the state legislature, in its infinite wisdom, forbade patrons from removing an unfinished bottle from the premises. You could take the bottle only if it was empty. If it retained a drop of wine you had to leave it behind. This was actually not so long ago – only about 20 years.

Those dark days are gone. You may now drink as much or as little from a bottle as you like, then tell the waiter that you want to take it with you along with any of your food leftovers. (For this reason be sure to retain the cork. Sometimes absentminded servers will take it away and dispose of it.) By law the bottle must be taken out in a paper bag or other container, but we know of no one who has ever been prosecuted by the state for failing in this weighty responsibility.

When Prohibition was repealed on 5 December, 1933, many vineyards were still producing (albeit table grapes), but the economic depression had reduced the demand for all but essentials. Wine was not high on the shopping list. A generation of winemakers had been lost. Few people knew about wine, or how to enjoy it. Beer was the most immediate demand, followed by whiskey. A few elderly ladies sought out sherry, old men looked for port, and the president of the United States shook martinis in the Oval Office. A daunting task lay ahead for those few remaining stalwarts of the ancient and honorable guild of vintners.

Things did not go well at first. In the early 1930s a Californian landowner could realize a better profit growing prunes rather than wine grapes. Also, a winemaker's wine could realize no immediate profit. This was an unattractive proposition in the depths of the Great Depression. A small number managed to hang on, and a few newcomers arrived on the scene. No doubt they were thought to be mad. They surely were mad for their craft and their product, for if it were only money they were after they might have been better off growing oranges in the Central Valley. And this distinguishes California's wine industry. Since the day of repeal in 1933 it has been a labor of love. Vineyardists and vintners have practiced their crafts with the dedication of an opera character who lives in a Parisian garret and suffers for his or her art. Many of them did suffer in the first decades. Even those larger and more successful operations were often land rich and cash poor. It was never certain that the American drinking public would turn to wine in great numbers. Even today most of the nation has a beer and booze (spirits) culture. We have no argument with beer or booze – they have their honorable place. But it was fortunate that California's wine culture never quite died in those dark days of Prohibition, and in the hard years after.

Things began to pick up in the 1950s and 60s. Departing from European tradition, Californians began to label their wines by grape variety (eg, zinfandel, sauvignon blanc) rather than by style or region (eg,

---

CONTINUING EDUCATION

The University of California has long played an important role in California's wine industry and culture. The campus at Davis, California, is the best known for producing graduates in enology, and in carrying out research. In 1938 this institution developed the "Heat Summation System," a process of determining the vineyard sustainability of a given piece of ground. Heat summation takes the measure of the total time the temperature rises above 50°F from 1 April to 31 October, and renders the figure in "degree days." For example, if over a five-day span the mean temperature is 70°F the summation would be (70 − 50 = 20) x 5 = 100 degree days. Using heat summation, any spot of ground can be classified as one of five climatic types. Most of the Golden State's premium wines are grown in the cooler type I and II regions.

Type I	2,500 or fewer degree days
Type II	2,501 to 3,000 degree days
Type III	3,001 to 3,500 degree days
Type IV	3,501 to 4,000 degree days
Type V	more than 4,000 degree days

This is certainly not the only tool for determining the suitability of a plot of earth to the vine, but it marks an important advancement in the science of this art.

The university is not alone in efforts at education. Many of the state's community colleges offer courses in wine appreciation, as do private schools, restaurants, and wineries. One of the newer and larger efforts is the American Institute of Wine, Food & the Arts, known as COPIA (see its website at Ⓦ www.copia.org), in the town of Napa. This is one of those mighty projects of outreach championed by superstar winemaker Robert Mondavi. It showcases California's gastronomy and oenology in a context of the fine arts. When in Napa, COPIA is well worth a visit.

DRINKS

Burgundy, Chablis). This had been done before, but rarely. This step was not without controversy, and was not universally accepted. But those wine-growers who were putting their heart and soul into the noble varieties were steadfast. Nowadays people take varietal labeling for granted, and Californians often ask what's in a Médoc or a Chianti. They have come to imbue the greatest meaning to the grape, not to the region or the style. To be labeled a varietal, California law requires that a wine be composed of not less than 75% of one grape variety. But content of 95% is not uncommon, and 100% is by no means unheard of.

An important development in the recovery of California's wine industry was the rise of the Gallo family. Brothers Earnest and Julio were the sons of Italian immigrants who manufactured wine. Between them, the brothers had a genius for production and a genius for marketing. In a short time, Gallo became the world's single largest producer of wine. Gallo is so

massive that there aren't any producers, anywhere in the world, who rank a close second in size. Its main winery in the Central Valley resembles an oil refinery with a characteristic tank farm. In addition to its own vast acreages, Gallo has always relied to a great extent on the excellent grapes of the Napa Valley, and later of Sonoma. This has had two important results: maintaining the price of grapes in California, making it predictable and high enough for producers to make a reasonable profit; and helping to establish a quality benchmark for Californian wines. Until recently Gallo made only jug wines (aka plonk). And while they included lesser grape varieties from the less prestigious Central Valley, they were blended with the superior fruit of Napa and Sonoma. This produced *vins ordinair* (cheap, ordinary wines) that were better than their counterparts anywhere in the world. And because Gallo is so huge and distributes everywhere in the state, no one dares offer anything less in quality.

Napa Valley, long and narrow, known far and wide.

DRINKS

BY THE GLASS

The serving of still and sparkling wine by the glass is now commonplace. Some restaurants offer only a few choices, perhaps half a dozen. Others vie with one another for by-the-glass glory. Typically you'll find at least a dozen fine selections in three-ounce offerings. Then there are those that offer 30, 80, or even 100 wines by the glass. As a rule of thumb, the larger places are able to offer more variety by the glass. But hey, isn't a choice of 30 enough?

The benchmark of quality and the drive to extract the last measure of goodness from premium varietals paid off in 1976 in a moment that has entered Californian legend: the Paris Tasting. At this "World Cup of Wine," two Californian upstarts, in blind tastings, beat out all their French rivals and were acclaimed as the best in the world. The Stag's Leap cabernet sauvignon and the Chateau Montelena chardonnay came home crowned with laurel, and California has been basking in glory ever since.

The famed cabernet sauvignon, Stag's Leap Wine Cellars, Napa

Aging oak wood for Swanson Winery, Oakville

California's ever-growing wine world has produced colorful personalities, just as every other sector of Californian life does. Andre Tschelitscheff found himself on the losing side of the Russian civil war following the Communist revolution. So he went to the former Yugoslavia to learn winemaking, worked a while in France, then came to California upon the repeal of Prohibition. Here he worked at Beaulieu in Napa and produced what is widely accepted as one of the finest wines the Golden State has ever produced: Georges de Latour Private Reserve cabernet sauvignon. Then there's Brother Timothy of the Christian Brothers, a monastic Catholic teaching order, who built the massive stone winery that now houses the CIA (Culinary Institute of America – see the boxed text Continuing Education, p30). The Gallo family have so many fat, delicious scandals that they were part of the inspiration for a TV series, a prime-time soap opera.

Perhaps the Californian love of flamboyant characters has helped give rise to what some people complain is a "cult of the winemaker." Everybody wants to be the friend of a winemaker, or to be a winemaker. Wealthy doctors, lawyers, brokers, movie makers, and recording artists are wont to purchase vineyards, and plant this or that, and grow the crop the way their fave winemaker has done. The cult of the winemaker has also resulted in a habit (among those with more money than is good for them) of paying more than $1,000 at auction for a bottle of chardonnay that in a blind tasting might be overvalued at $24.95. Californians have become used to being soaked when buying the labels of a popular winemaker.

DRINKS

CORKAGE

It is common for Californians to bring a special wine from their own collection to a restaurant. Perhaps it was a birthday gift, or an acquisition from a trip to Europe or Australia, or Oregon or Washington. Or maybe you're flying in to California with a sample from your native land. Welcome to the Golden State, enjoy your special wine, and pay the corkage fee. "Corkage" refers to the nominal fee paid to the wine steward for pulling the cork from your special bottle. Not long ago, Californian corkage fees were a pittance. Three dollars was common. Considering that restaurant prices for wine are about 100% over retail, this made for a good bargain. Unfortunately, too many people realized that and brought their own on a regular basis. Restaurateurs accordingly jacked up the corkage fee. These days in the better establishments you can expect to pay at least $10 corkage, and $30 is not unheard of. Our advice is to call ahead and ask.

LA Prime Steakhouse, Westin Bonaventure Hotel, Los Angeles

Maybe it's time to remind the Californians that in Europe there isn't even a name for winemaker, let alone a cult status for such a person. So when you visit California, don't be blinded by prestigious labels – remember that even the cheap stuff is good stuff. And there are discount dealers to run to for refuge. Two good examples are Beverages & More, and Smart & Final. Find them in the telephone book. Many wineries offer free guided tours with a visit to the tasting room. Some charge a small fee to enter the tasting room, just to keep the freeloaders at bay.

Red roses add color to the vineyard

Wining & Dining on the Wine Country Trail

One of the things that drives California Cuisine is the desire of chefs to take advantage of the wealth of wine, and to pair the liquid food with the solid. Many chefs make a specialty of this, especially those in the wine country. Their efforts have produced a multitude of famous houses of good eats and drinks. While most of them are on the pricey side, they are definitely worth a splurge.

One of the most emblematic, both of Californian wine and Californian food is Martini House in Saint Helena. (The locals say saint hel-**ee**-na.) The restaurant's name has nothing to do with the cocktail, though you may find a good one there. It's named after Walter Martini, a San Francisco opera singer who retired about the time of Prohibition. He built the house that the restaurant now occupies, and is said to have run an illicit still in the basement. After visits to the basement he would emerge onto the front lawn and serenade the neighborhood.

The house has since been redesigned and is operated by Pat Kuleto. He is far and away California's most celebrated restaurant designer, and is a respected winemaker. The service, food (California Cuisine), wine, and décor are all world-class. But because this is California none of it intimidates. Even if you've saved your pennies for weeks in order to come here just for

WINE COUNTRY TRAIL

Lake Berryessa
Bothe-Napa Valley State Park
Deer Park
Spanish Flat
128
St Helena
1
Lake Hennessey
128
Rutherford
2
Sugarloaf Ridge State Park
Oakville
NAPA VALLEY
Kenwood
Trinity Rd
Yountville
3
Napa River
Annadel State Park
Glen Ellen
Jack London State Historic Park
12
SONOMA VALLEY
California
29
Agua Caliente
Penngrove
El Verano
Sonoma
4
Napa

0   3   6 km
0   1.5   3 mi

Recommended Restaurants

1. Martini House
   1245 Spring Street, Saint Helena

2. Auberge du Soleil
   180 Rutherford Hill Road, Rutherford

3. French Laundry
   6640 Washington Street, Yountville

4. Carneros
   1325 Broadway, Sonoma

lunch, they'll gladly stash your backpack and make you feel at home. Significantly, the staff are all extremely well versed in the wines on offer, and you would do very well to let them look after all your food–wine pairings. Or if you want to start with something other than wine, we think they pour the best iced tea under the sun. Really! You'll find Martini House at 1245 Spring Street, Saint Helena.

Other well-regarded wine country eateries include:

Auberge du Soleil
French technique and sensibility brought to bear on a local and seasonal ingredient-driven menu.
180 Rutherford Hill Road, Rutherford
☎ 707-963-1211

French Laundry
Big food done delicately. A two-month wait for reservations, and it's worth it.
6640 Washington Street, Yountville
☎ 707-944-2380

Carneros
Splashy décor and an "artisan wine country cuisine" that should be read as luxurious and a bit fattening, in a good way.
1325 Broadway, Sonoma
☎ 707-931-2042

DRINKS

SCREW YOU?

There is increasing awareness among serious winemakers that the world's supply of cork oak is finite. Many experiments are underway to find alternatives to the ancient practice of sealing wine bottles with a cork plug. Two avenues of approach have emerged. One is the use of synthetic corks – this holds much promise, but is yet to be proven. The other is the use of plastic screw caps, often with a thin cork gasket – this is becoming more and more accepted, and may become the norm. But it begs the question: if you bring your own wine to the restaurant in a screw-cap bottle, will they charge you screwage?

Cheers either way

Wine Regions & Varieties

Wine can be grown virtually anywhere in California. But there are certain designated growing zones called American Viticultural Areas (AVAs). These are similar to the French system of *Appellation D'Origine Contrôlée* (AOC), though are not as meaningful. They are defined only by geographical criteria; they have no bearing on quality, variety, production, or alcohol levels. They can be large or small; straddle county lines; contain sub-AVAs; overlap each other; and be sensibly defined or seem to be a winemaker's dry joke. At the time of writing there are roughly 80 AVAs within the state, and the number is sure to rise. By no means are all wines grown within designated AVAs. Most Californian consumers just check to see that the label bears the name of California or of the Californian county in which at least 75% of the wine is grown. Californians generally think variety first, then county (cult winemaker notwithstanding).

Above: Cabernet grape harvest, Napa Valley
Left: A fine day for grape harvesting

DRINKS

WINE REGIONS

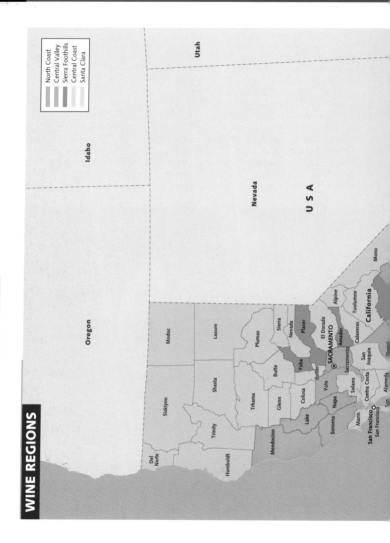

Legend:
- North Coast
- Central Valley
- Sierra Foothills
- Central Coast
- Santa Clara

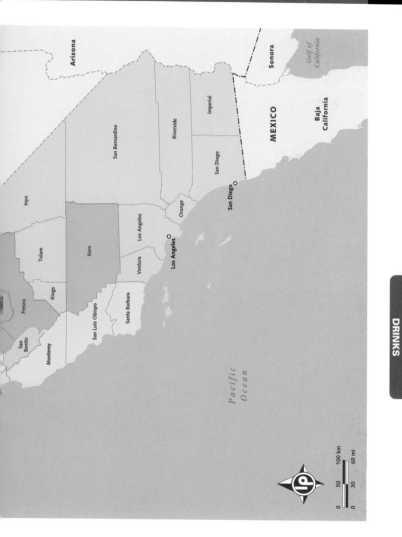

Napa County

Widely held to be the heart of California's wine world, the Napa Valley is geographically rather small. Though it has a length of some 30 miles the valley narrows to as little as one mile, and is only four miles at its widest. Yet it contains such a wide range of microclimates that it can mirror the entire weather spectrum of the wine regions of France. Virtually the whole of Napa County falls under the AVA of "Napa Valley." There are about 200 wineries here, though many of them are tiny "boutique" or "vanity" operations producing as little as 1,000 cases per year. By far the most common grapes grown here are cabernet sauvignon and chardonnay. Zinfandel is common, as well as pinot noir, chenin blanc, gewürztraminer, and the list goes on. The most famous names in wine are here: Mondavi, Beaulieu, the sparklers Mumm's and Schramsburg, and those victors of the Paris Tasting – Stag's Leap and Chateau Montelena.

Napa Valley is one of the most beautiful growing regions and is a popular tourist destination, especially with weekend day-trippers. For that reason you should try to visit on a weekday. Not only does it get crowded on weekends, but there is only one road (Highway 29) going through it, with two lanes. It can back up for miles. If you visit from the San Francisco area, consider spending the night, continuing on northward, or at least not returning till late. The daily afternoon commuter traffic is horrid.

Wind machines for frost control, Napa Valley

Sonoma County

While Sonoma County has produced wine since the 19th century (indeed, before Napa), it is a relative newcomer to the modern industry, at least for premium varietals. Before about 1970 it produced mostly jug wine. More land was dedicated to orchards than to wine. Now Sonoma grows more chardonnay than Napa, as well as zinfandel and pinot noir. Like Napa, it has a wide range of climatic regions. AVAs of Sonoma include Alexander Valley, Chalk Hills, and Russian River Valley. Sonoma shares the famous Carneros AVA, famous for its pinot noir, with Napa County. Some of the best-known labels of Sonoma include Souverain, Simi, and Sebastiani.

Sonoma is a superb place for a day trip, or in which to spend a few days in a resort. It's easy to drive to and around, and is blessed with lovely oak- and vine-covered country scenery, and a lot of history. It was in the little town of Sonoma that General Vallejo found himself the unexpected guest of the revelers of 1846 (see p12). Sonoma's central plaza is a great place for a picnic.

WARNING LABEL

American wine labels must carry two warnings to the consumer. One is that alcohol could be dangerous to your health or to your unborn child. The other, if applicable (and it usually is) is that the wine contains sulfites. Sulfites are not ingredients in wine, they are processing agents customarily used to control fermentation. When the wine has finished fermentation there can be infinitesimally small trace amounts of sulfites remaining. Some people with hypersensitivity to sulfites have been known to be irritated by them. So now you've been warned. Cheers!

DRINKS

Mendocino County

Immediately north of Sonoma County, Mendocino stretches along the coast for 100 miles, but most of its wine is grown in the southern third. Chardonnay, zinfandel, and cabernet sauvignon are the dominant varieties here, as well as gewürtztraminer, petit sirah, and carignane. AVAs include the highly regarded Anderson Valley, Cole Ranch, Potter Valley, and Redwood Valley. Mendocino County's climate is as varied as Sonoma's, but in general is cooler. Mendocino is too far from San Francisco for a day trip, but it's a very popular weekend getaway destination. The coastal highway is a gorgeous drive, and the many state beaches provide perfect picnic spots.

Santa Clara County

Located at the southern end of San Francisco Bay, this county is also known as Silicon Valley. Industry and housing have pushed vineyards further and further south, so you'll have to go as far as Gilroy or Hecker Pass to reach them. The most important AVA is Santa Clara Valley. The common grape varieties are chardonnay, cabernet sauvignon, and zinfandel. While the county's acreage under vines has decreased in recent years, there are still 25 wineries operating here. They include famous names like Mirassou, Paul Masson, and J. Lohr. In the Hecker Pass area along Route 152 are several small family wineries, which most people are unaware of, but which are definitely worth a visit.

DRINKS

Cabernet sauvignon grapes

Central Valley Counties

More than three-quarters of California's total wine production comes from the huge Central Valley. A drive along Highway 99 can be stunning. Vineyards stretch out to the horizon in some places. There are vineyards that are larger than many towns. The Central Valley is strictly an agricultural zone, so it doesn't draw many tourists. Therefore, you should make an effort to visit. Some important counties are Merced, Stanislaus, and Madera. AVAs include Madera, Clarksburg, and Merritt Island. This is a hot place, and heat inhibits the development of essential acids in wine grapes, so the varieties grown here tend to be those that would develop very high acid content in cooler climes. Colombard and chenin blanc are common white varieties. Zinfandel seems to do well almost anywhere here, and grenache, barbera, and carignane grapes cover vast territories.

Sierra Foothills Counties

Immediately north of the Central Valley, this is zinfandel land. Zinfandel is by far the most widely planted grape here in the "Gold Country." Counties include Yuba, Placer, Mariposa, and especially Amador. Close to 40 wineries dot these rising lands that lead to the High Sierra. Famous AVAs include Fiddletown and Shenandoah Valley. A bit of cabernet comes from here, as well as chardonnay and sauvignon blanc. But mainly, it's zinfandel. And the mountain scenery is pretty dramatic. This is excellent territory for a wine weekend.

Zinfandel grapes just before harvest

DRINKS

Central Coast Counties

The territory running south from the San Francisco Bay almost to Los Angeles makes up a huge, single AVA called Central Coast. There are many sub-AVAs within this AVA. It includes the coastal counties of Santa Cruz, Monterey, San Louis Obispo, and Santa Barbara. Any wine made of more than one AVA in this zone will be labeled Central Coast. What such a disparate collection of territories has in common is plentiful sunlight – this would normally mean high temperatures, but the sea breeze exerts a cooling influence. The Humboldt Current running up the Californian shore is quite cold and affects the weather of the shoreline zones. A lot of chardonnay, a lover of cool weather, is grown here, especially in Monterey County, which also produces more than half the state's crop of pinot blanc. Monterey reds are said to have a pleasing "vegetative" aroma reminiscent of sweet pepper. Almost all wines of Monterey are under the Monterey AVA. Chardonnay is also dominant in Santa Barbara County, and shares top spot

Chardonnay grapes just before harvest

with cabernet sauvignon in San Louis Obispo County. Other common varieties of the Central Coast include riesling, chenin blanc, zinfandel, and what many will argue is the best pinot noir in the state, grown in the Chalone sub-AVA near Soledad. The Central Coast embraces the area known as Big Sur, one of the most beautiful coastal drives anywhere in America. A winery trip through this area should be allotted several days.

Beer

In 1848 the entire world, or so it might have seemed, converged on California in pursuit of gold. In their lust for lucre they dug deep holes in the virgin ground, panned the snow-fed rivers, picked at the rocks of unforgiving mountains, shot away soil with huge jets of water, and shot each other with six-guns over mining claims. Thirsty work. In addition to the demand for Levi Strauss' riveted trousers, the pickaxes and gold pans, food, tents, and blasting powder essential to their pursuit of the golden metal, they thirsted for the golden brew.

> "You can't be a real country unless you have a beer and an airline – it helps if you have some kind of a football team, or some nuclear weapons, but at the very least you need a beer."
>
> *Frank Zappa*

Midwestern brewers saw their chance at creating wealth from the wealth seekers. In those days, lager was the preferred brew in America, and the Midwestern brewers of states like Wisconsin and Illinois were producing mass quantities for distribution far and wide. A necessity of the lager process is low temperature, and the Midwestern brewers were able to achieve this almost year-round due to the ice trade on the Great Lakes. The winter ice from this region was chopped or sawn into manageable chunks, packed in sawdust, and sent all over the central states. It was an industry that thrived into the 20th century. But in the days of horse and dray anyone who tried to ship ice from Chicago to San Francisco would arrive with a load of drinking water. So it seemed lager would always be brewed in the colder Midwest.

However, enterprising brewers in San Francisco hit upon an idea that was stunning in its simplicity. They could use a lager recipe, with a lager-style yeast, but brew the beer as one would an ale, in ale-brewing vessels and at higher temperature. The result was a brew with a rich, malty aroma and an assertive taste, that was full bodied, though not so much as a porter. It was crisp and dry like a lager, yet with the fullness of an ale. It also had such an effervescence that when the keg was tapped it billowed off a cloud of mist resembling steam. Hence its name to this day: "steam beer."

Steam beer is the only indigenous American beer. As far as we know it is made nowhere outside the USA, although it is exported to Canada and the UK. It is also made nowadays in many other American states, though it is known there as "California Common." All steam beer is artisanal beer, made by hand in smaller breweries. It is unlikely major brewers would ever care to create and mass market this stuff. With so many American beer drinkers being seduced by light beer, or other mild brews, the robust flavor of a good steam beer is thought by marketeers as just too much for the increasingly homogenous national palate.

DRINKS

The chief exponent and producer of steam beer today is the Anchor Brewing Company, in San Francisco, established in 1896. The Maytag family, who first prospered in the excellent state of Iowa, where they made and sold a very fine cheese, began a business of manufacturing and distributing washing machines. They were hugely successful, and became known as much for their clever TV commercials as for their products. Fritz Maytag, a scion of the vastly enriched family, came to California in the 1960s as a university student, and sampled steam beer. He was instantly seduced, as had been the 49ers of old.

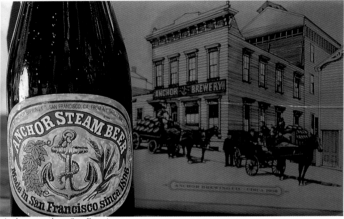

Anchor steam beer, San Francisco

Alas, California's steam-beer breweries of the mid-20th century had been falling left and right, as casualties in the marketing wars with larger battalions of lesser brews. By the time Fritz Maytag had quaffed his first mug of Golden State amber, the Anchor brewery was the last of California's steam-beer breweries. As his student days grew to a close, so did the days of Anchor Brewing. Fritz couldn't bear to see the loss of such a worthy contribution to human happiness. So he cashed all of his shares in the family fortune, and as a young man who knew nothing of beer but what he loved, acquired the ancient and honorable, though poor and dilapidated, brewery that didn't even have bottling capabilities. All Anchor sold then was on draft, and that was only to old geezers who knew its history and to young men who knew nothing but what they liked.

To cut a long story short, Fritz and a few employees turned the operation around. They modernized, they "bottlized," they "marketized." They moved from a dilapidated hovel under a freeway overpass into an elegant building that once housed an important coffee concern. They acquired new, shiny copper equipment. Perhaps most importantly, they reminded the Californians of their history and the fact that they could drink it.

Today Anchor Steam is the most popular steam beer anywhere. It is easily recognized in a glass – its color is a distinct dark amber, and its head is so thick and creamy that it resembles zabaglione. Or, if you prefer, custard. It is triple-hopped, and fully malted, so its assertive taste and rich aroma make it the perfect foil for barbecued food, chile con carne, Cal-Mex dishes, or a delicious sunset on the Californian coast. The story of Anchor is one that all beer-drinking Californians take pleasure in, as it reaffirms their belief that they live in "The Best Place on Earth."

But steam beer is just the beginning, not the end, of beer in California. Ron Silberstein, one of the owners of the ThirstyBear Brewing Company (brewpub and restaurant) in San Francisco, points out that California is a focus of world brewing. All manner of styles are to be had here. "But that's not the most important thing," he says.

"While we recognize the various styles and regions, we aren't bound by them. Rather than think style and region, we just think 'beer.' We aren't limited by style and region. Like wine, and California Cuisine, beer has an infinite range of expression. We're always trying new things, as well as the old standbys. What we're after is for the drinker to be able to say, with eyes closed, 'This is a fine beer, but like nothing I've ever had before.'"

Californians love their suds

DRINKS

Beers made in California are simply too numerous to name. But you will have no problem finding them. Simply look in the telephone directory under beer, brewery, or brewpub. Perhaps the biggest might be the Yard House restaurant in SoCal (Southern California). This place (now with five locations: Long Beach, Costa Mesa, Irvine, Rancho Mirage, and San Diego) has the world's largest range of draught beer. If you like, they will serve one to you in a glass exactly one yard long. Residents of England may be familiar with yard-long glasses, and with contests where you drink from them. Should you be feeling competitive, you will have no problem finding someone to accept your challenge.

Ron Silberstein (center) and Richard Sterling (right) at a tasting, ThirstyBear, San Francisco

Cocktails
The Martini

It became the drink of choice for literati such as Jack London and Henry Miller, and the official drink of the ruling class and those who would aspire to it. Franklin D.

> "I must get out of these wet clothes and into a dry martini."
>
> *Robert Benchley in* China Seas *(MGM)*

Roosevelt (FDR) and Winston Churchill mixed their own to the definitive recipe, while James Bond gave detailed instructions to the barkeep for a somewhat idiosyncratic mix. It is the bibulous symbol of America; it is pure California and the signature drink of San Francisco. Not bad for a dram that began in a sawdust saloon.

As the story goes, it was in 1862 that the famous "Professor" Jerry Thomas concocted the first martini. He was the head bartender at San Francisco's Occidental Hotel on Montgomery Street, where he daily attended to the needs of his "patients." A traveler whose name is lost to history entered the bar and told the Professor that he was proceeding to the nearby town of Martinez and that he need fortitude for the journey. Seizing the moment, the good Prof put together a mixture of gin, vermouth, and some other bits and bobs and proclaimed the drink the Martinez Cocktail. The recipe for this potion later appeared in Jerry's best-selling book, *The Bon Vivant's Companion, or How to Mix Drinks*. Other well-known creations by Thomas also are included in the book, such as the Tom & Jerry and the flaming Blue Blazer.

All San Franciscans know the truth of the martini's origin, though there are liars and boasters elsewhere who dispute this truth. There are Brits who patriotically claim that the drink is named for the Martini & Henry rifle employed by Her Majesty's armies in the late 19th century. However, they cannot say when or where the drink appeared, only that it has a kick comparable to the rifle. And there is a stubborn lot in that nearby town of Martinez who maintain that their little spot on the map is the true site of the origin. But when dueling pistols are produced they are wont to retreat.

Despite differences over origin, we all agree that the estimable martini began as a quite different drink than today's. Thomas' recipe calls for a gin known as Old Tom, a sweetened London gin. It also calls for vermouth to equal about one-third of the volume. By the 1890s, however, the mix had become much drier, with the Old Tom being replaced with a dry gin, but it still contained one-third vermouth and would remain so for decades.

By the mid-20th century, martini aficionados were demanding drier and yet drier drinks. (The same was true for wines as well as cocktails.) By the end of WWII the standard martini was being mixed at a ratio of about

10:1, gin to vermouth. Those who desired a very dry martini took it at 15:1 and would ask for a Monty. This was a sly dig at the British field marshal Bernard Montgomery, of WWII fame. He was known for being cautious, and his detractors said of him that he would never attack the enemy until he outnumbered it 15:1.

By the 1960s the martini had become little more than a chilled glass of gin with a mere insinuation of French vermouth, usually Noilly Prat. The decade also saw the advent of atomizers with which to spray the glass with a gossamer mist of the French stuff. Some mixologists took to the "rinse," where they poured a bit of vermouth into the glass, swirled it around and poured it out. Those with a greater sense of the theatrical merely bowed towards France in homage to the vermouth, without adding a drop, then slugged in the gin.

Then came James Bond. And vodka. Gin is little more than vodka that has been flavored with juniper berries and anywhere from six to 18 other "botanicals." Vermouth starts as an unremarkable white wine that is flavored with wormwood and many other botanicals. So many competing herbaceous tastes and aromas can be a bit much for the modern palate. Enter 007. He softened the mix with a splash of the neutral taste of a finely distilled vodka. The idea caught on, the vodka component increased, and for many martini drinkers it wasn't long before the gin was entirely displaced. The vodka martini has actually gained recognition, even in San Francisco, but the gin martini remains constant.

The garnish for the martini is an item of much dispute. Patricians claim that only a Spanish olive is acceptable. Iconoclasts demand a lemon peel, twisted over the drink to express its oil onto the surface of the liquid, then rubbed on the rim of the glass. (Jerry Thomas' original recipe called for a slice of lemon dropped into the drink.) If using the olive, adding a splash of olive brine produces what is known as a dirty martini. FDR was said to favor this. Garnishing with a small pickled onion renders the drink entirely anew and it is then called a Gibson.

Nowhere more than San Francisco is the martini considered a protected species. Its most elegant and ceremonial service is at the Compass Rose bar in the Westin Saint Francis hotel. But even the most untutored barkeep in the most degraded dive in the Tenderloin district can render a proper martini when called upon. There are NorCal (Northern California) folk who will drink but one martini a year, yet demand perfection. It just goes with the territory. But then there is LA.

When you journey to La-La Land you will find the martini landscape loony by San Francisco standards. You may have a martini in LA, Hollywood, Brentwood, and Beverly Hills. Every bar and disco will offer them. Indeed, your server will produce the house's "martini menu." This

Three flavors of martini at the Compass Rose, Westin St Francis, San Francisco

Classic martini

is usually a list of drinks (some very appetizing) that incorporate no gin and no vermouth. They may use chocolate, coffee, or green tea. The alcohol may be Mexican mescal, Polish vodka, or even Japanese sake. It might even be served in a martini glass, a tumbler, or a beer glass, on the rocks or not. It may have a pair of straws in it, or a paper umbrella. It might be finished with a dollop of sparkling wine! In Los Angeles, you see, a martini is anything the bartender calls a martini. If you want the real thing in Hollywood, well, it is Hollywood, where some people say there is no such thing as a real thing.

So when you go to a Californian bar and order a martini, how should you do so? If you want the genuine article, instruct the barkeep thus: pour Bombay or Boodles generously over ice in a cocktail shaker. Give it a good splash of vermouth. Maybe half an ounce. Make it a cocktail, not a straight shot. Keep in mind that the opposite of dry is not wet, but sweet (most bartenders these days do not know this – here is your opportunity to perform a public service and educate them). Now shake it into submission. Shake it till it cries for mercy. Shake it so that the botanicals volatilize and reveal themselves to your senses while still remaining glacially cold. Shake it so that when you pour it into a chilled glass, ice crystals float upon the surface. Now garnish. Now taste. Mmmm. Perfection.

Irish Coffee

Irish coffee has become so identified with San Francisco that many people assume it was invented there, and they will even cite the Buena Vista Cafe near Fisherman's Wharf as the inventor's laboratory (keep reading to find out why). It is a perfect drink for The City as it lies draped in its chilly fog. The blend of piping-hot coffee and blood-stirring Irish whiskey is what makes sidewalk dining and drinking possible for half the year. That and the outdoor heat lamps, of course. Walk down Broadway or Columbus Avenue on any typical (read: chilly) evening and you will see table after table bearing the distinctive long-stemmed glasses that are considered essential for the proper enjoyment of this gut-warming drink. At the aforementioned Buena Vista Cafe the cry of "Make one!" from a waiter is understood to be an order for the Irish. However, it is more common to hear higher numbers called. In Bar Tosca, with its famous jukebox full of opera selections, the bar is always lined with Irish coffee glasses charged with whiskey, sugar, and cream, simply awaiting a helping of hot coffee (a variation on the usual recipe, which adds the cream last).

From whence came the Celtic concoction? We really don't know. But we're of the opinion that the Irish have been showing kindness to coffee in this way ever since coffee arrived on the Emerald Isle. And before coffee they were showing kindness to tea, water, and anything else deemed to require that special form of Irish generosity. But we can say for certain how it came into the consciousness of San Franciscans.

Newspaper columnist and bon vivant Stanton Delaplane made a trip to Ireland in 1952. At Shannon Airport he met and befriended bartender Joe Sheridan. In the chill of the Irish mist, much like the chill of the San Francisco fog, he saw many a patron stop by to warm the cockles of their hearts with what at first appeared to be a small glass of stout, but on closer inspection was seen to be sweetened coffee with whiskey, and a foamy head of cream. Delaplane tried it, liked it, and brought the idea for it home to Jack Koeppler, the Buena Vista's head mixmeister. After a bit of trial and error they learned that to keep the cream from sinking into the drink, they had to whip it very slightly, then gently pour it into the glass over an upturned spoon. It was an immediate success.

Irish Coffee

Ingredients

1 jigger (1–2 oz/30–60mL)	Irish whiskey
	piping-hot, fresh-filtered coffee (enough to fill your long-stemmed glass)
1 tsp	brown sugar
¼ cup (60mL)	heavy (whipping) cream, slightly whipped

Preheat the serving glass by filling with hot water, then emptying it. Pour the coffee into the glass until it is about three-quarters full, then stir in the brown sugar until it is completely dissolved. Pour in the Irish whiskey from a height of about six inches above the glass, so that it blends thoroughly. Place an upturned tablespoon over the top of the glass, making sure the edge of the spoon is in contact with the inside of the glass. Top the coffee by gently pouring the cream over the spoon. Do not stir the cream through the drink.

Serves 1

The Margarita

The exact origin of the margarita is lost and unrecoverable to humanity. However, we know that it originally followed the Mexican way of taking tequila. The *cantinero* pours the thirsty *campesino* a generous shot of tequila, then serves up a wedge or two of fresh lime and a shaker of salt. Observing ritual, the patron of the bar licks his left wrist to moisten it, then sprinkles it with salt. Then he takes a sip (or knocks back the whole) of the tequila, licks up the salt, and takes a bite of lime. Or he may take lime and salt first, then wash it down with tequila. Either way is a short trip to a quick buzz.

Where and when somebody graced a hurricane glass with salt at the rim, then mixed the tequila and lime with ice, and threw in an inspired dash of orange liqueur, is anyone's guess. Most people subscribe to one of two legends:

Salted margarita, the classic version

1. Rita Hayworth (1940s film star) used to be a regular patron at a Hollywood bar run by Enrique Bastante Gutierez. According to Señor Gutierez, he mixed the drink especially for Miss Hayworth – she liked it and ordered it often. As an homage to the star he named it for her. Her real name was Margarita.

2. During the years of Prohibition, Tijuana in Mexico was Southern California's playground. On weekends half of Hollywood could be found there. Silent-screen siren Marjorie King was no exception, and was a regular at the Rancho La Gloria bar. It was said that she could drink only tequila, so barman Danny Herrera concocted many a potion for the celluloid diva. Her favorite was said to be one with lime and Cointreau, which Danny named for her. Margarita is the Spanish for Marjorie.

Take your choice of creation myths, or make up your own. No one could authoritatively call you a liar. It will never be known when or where or who created this luscious drink. But we can be confident that it was California that made the margarita first a custom and then a craze. We know for sure that the El Cholo restaurant of Los Angeles has been serving classic margaritas in huge volume for decades. As they do today. This drink is tequila, fresh lime juice, and Cointreau stirred together and then poured into a tall, ice-filled glass, its rim encrusted with coarse-grain salt. It is refreshing, appetizing, stimulating, and is bound to help to prevent heat exhaustion and scurvy.

Blended margarita

When blending machines became widely available, so did the frozen margarita, and seemingly innumerable variations of the recipe. Now we have margaritas made from almost any fruit, though the common ones are strawberry, mango, and papaya. These are quintessential "foo-foo" drinks, replete with paper umbrellas and sometimes served in a coconut shell or oversized cocktail glass. They are popular on the cruise ships that sail out of Los Angeles and San Diego.

But a real margarita, whether it be traditional or frozen, is a fine and respectable libation. Californians often prepare margaritas at home and serve them with guacamole and corn chips (see p51). Bars that specialize in margaritas often have blending machines, rather like beer taps, that dispense the frozen variety instantly on demand. The margarita is a drink for both high and low (and most Californians consider themselves to be both). It can precede a fine Mexican dinner, accompany a ball game on TV, or even be enjoyed amid the vineyards of Napa Valley, and nowhere will a discouraging word be heard about it.

DRINKS

Non-Alcoholic Drinks
Coffee

Coffee runs along two tracks in California. There is the workaday coffee that people buy in the supermarket, and there is the traditional American "coffee shop," a place where people go to eat simple food more than to drink coffee. They might not drink coffee at all in a coffee shop. And if they do it will be that same ordinary stuff found in the supermarket. There is, however, an emerging "coffee culture." This is despite Californians showing, to the consternation of purists, an increased preference for sweet, frothy, milky concoctions that might be more suited to the soda fountain or ice-cream parlor. But in the better restaurants, unalloyed and unadorned espresso and filter coffees are the norm.

California's coffee culture began with Dutch immigrant Alfred Peet in 1966. He had worked in Indonesia for his family's coffee and tea company, and had a great knowledge of coffee, great skill at roasting, and a passion for a better bean. He opened his first little roastery in Berkeley, around the corner from where Alice Waters would open Chez Panisse five years later (see p16). The simple and efficient shop still looks much the same, and patrons still take their coffee out to the shaded sidewalk to enjoy it. There are now over 60 Peet's Coffee & Tea outlets, and you'll find them in both NorCal and SoCal, as well as interstate.

Finding a caffeine hit in California should be no problem

It wasn't long before Peet's Coffee & Tea gave birth to another company. In 1970 two of Peet's roasters left for Seattle and started a little outfit called Starbucks. Maybe you've heard of it. If you haven't, you will soon. It now has more than 2,000 outlets and it continues to expand. But things have come full circle, in a way. One of the Starbucksters decided to sell out in 1987 – he then came back home to California and bought Peet's.

Peet's retail stores serve a great cup of joe, but the company is on a mission to roast and sell "the best coffee beans on the planet." As with the more solid food of California Cuisine, freshness is paramount. Peet's orders beans for roasting up to five times a week, and coffee not sold within two weeks is donated to local charities.

Though Peet's is now a publicly traded company, it has a great number of independent imitators. Most are lone operations, and a few are small chains. You'll find them especially concentrated near university campuses (espresso would seem to be the official drink of students). Coffee outlets are also plentiful in shopping and entertainment districts. Along Highway 1 you'll pass one every now and then in the little towns that dot the coast. You'll also find them on Highway 80, the route to Lake Tahoe.

Tea

Ever since the Boston Tea Party, where colonial American tax protesters hurled mad King George's tea into the harbor in 1773, Americans from coast to coast have generally favored coffee over tea. If you are visiting from Japan or China or even Britain you will be exasperated by the quality of tea on offer in supermarkets. And in the average restaurant the tea service consists of a little pot of indifferently heated water, a cup cold enough to suck even more heat from the water, and a bag of supermarket tea. It appears the Americans are still pissed off at King George.

The various Chinatowns, Japantowns, and Koreatowns have always had a good supply and the knowledge of what to do with it. But the general population has been as tepid toward it as the water in the restaurant service. There are still men in the US who consider tea a lady's drink. But things are changing in California. As life gets more frenetic and the afternoon traffic more impossible, people are looking for ways to slow down, to calm their nerves without benefit of controlled substances, and to enjoy quiet company. Tea, with its reduced caffeine levels and perhaps more refined allure, offers an alternative to coffee. Californians also enjoy herbal teas, just as many do throughout the nation, and they are plentiful in supermarkets.

Peet's, of coffee fame, also sells and promotes tea. But the chief purveyor of specialty teas (the only ones worth drinking) is a company called The Republic of Tea, established in 1992. It promotes not only the drinking of tea, but the contemplative, even ceremonial enjoyment of the brew. They

Flavored teas from The Republic of Tea

have many small imitators who teach and conduct various tea ceremonies. Some of the more dedicated devotees of ceremonial tea drinking don't even call it an indulgence or an enjoyment, but the practicing of an art. Dedicated coffee drinkers generally have a different opinion.

Be that as it may, there is a growing interest in tea in California. Many of the grand hotels offer a British-style "high tea" in the afternoon. Some are offered daily, some weekly. But that style is a bit heavy for many Californians. The Golden State faces Asia, not England. And maybe the ghost of King George still haunts. In the last decade, Asian-style tearooms have been opening, including the Imperial Tea Court in San Francisco, the American School of Japanese Arts in Santa Rosa, and L'Amyx Tea Bar in Oakland. The Ten Ren company also has several outlets around the state, selling a wide variety of teas, as well as serving it on premises. You can locate outlets through its website (**W** www.tenren.com).

The better restaurants now offer better tea. Chez Panisse even has its own tea sommelier. In any higher-class joint the staff will be able to intelligently advise you on a choice of tea. This being California, of course, few people will drink tea during the meal, preferring the grape or the barley. But tea is an increasingly popular after-dinner tipple.

One sort of tea that has long been popular in sunny California is sun tea. You put a cup of tea leaves in a one-gallon glass jar, fill with water, secure the lid, and place it in the sun for two to six hours, depending on the cloud cover. It often is the basis for afternoon iced tea (iced tea is as popular here as anywhere else in the nation, but if you're from the USA's south you may want to add sugar). Sun tea is traditional at picnics and ball games, and on lazy summer days. At housewares shops you can buy special handblown jars for creating this special tea.

Water

Bottled water is so plentiful in California that you could bathe in it and it wouldn't cost you much. A lot of it is imported stuff with fancy labels, and is referred to derisively as "designer water." Most of the native brew comes from NorCal. That's because SoCal doesn't have much, being largely desert. One of the most common, and one that enjoys great brand loyalty, is Calistoga water. It's bottled at Calistoga Springs, in the Wine Country, and is naturally sparkling. You can get it plain, or lightly flavored with essence of citrus.

Sculpture constructed of crates of bottles at Calistoga Mineral Water Company

DRINKS

DRINKS

Juice

With California as the fruit-and-vegetable basket of the nation, it should come as no surprise that Californians drink a lot of juice. Orange juice is far and away the most common type. For many years it came to market as frozen concentrate, then later as reconstituted frozen concentrate. But with the freshness revolution came a little company called Odwalla, originally in Santa Cruz but now located in the Central Valley. Its mission was to bring freshly squeezed fruit and vegetable juices to a mass market. This required a high degree of organization and transport because the juices had to be expressed, bottled, refrigerated, and sent to market within a matter of hours.

Come to California and get juiced

And the product has a very brief shelf life. But the taste of freshly squeezed juice caught on quickly, and Odwalla soon had imitators. Nowadays, in order to ensure a hygienic product, the juices are flash pasteurized – brought up to a high temperature very quickly and cooled down just as quickly. This keeps them safe and gives them a few more days of shelf life. This and the organization required makes them more expensive than reconstituted frozen concentrate, but you'll taste the difference.

home cooking
& traditions

Because of its ethnic diversity, California is a place of innumerable traditions, not the least of which is embracing new traditions. You'll find the past, present, and the future; the familiar and the far-flung; and the sacred and profane in the Californian home kitchen.

Step into a home kitchen in California and prepare for something of a shock. Perhaps you've seen restaurant kitchens up close. You know how filled they are with implementaria, culinaria, condimentia, and just dementia; as well as legions of staff and much chattering, clattering, and clanging. A home kitchen in the Golden State can be even more cluttered. With regular trips to Williams-Sonoma, pottery sheds, food boutiques, and wine merchants, Californians often have their kitchens stuffed to the rafters. And Mom, Dad, all the kids, and a few neighbors might be in there at the same time. Because maybe a home chef has come by to teach them baking, or menu planning, or roasting, or jam making. Or maybe they're just all cooking together. Californian kids often take part, as well as both parents. Indeed, it isn't uncommon for the man of the family to be the principal cook. And househusbands are not unknown.

A typically well-stocked Californian kitchen

Home Ingredients & Utensils

The Californian home kitchen will have more variety in its shelves than the restaurant, which usually specializes in one type of cookery, with one set of spices, oils, condiments, etc. The home cook, on the other hand, is interested in everything. The spice rack contains a lot more than just parsley, sage, rosemary, and thyme. It holds cans of coconut cream as well as olive oil, walnut oil, avocado oil, and unsalted butter, Thai or Vietnamese fermented fish sauce, oyster sauce, a kaleidoscope of chile sauces, and, yes, Worcestershire sauce.

Braids of garlic hang from the wall, as do *ristras* (strings) of all kinds of braided chile peppers, from little red serranos to big brown pasillas, smoky chipotles to mild green New Mexicans. Shelves hold apothecary jars full of pasta. Sweet spices such as star anise, cardamom, allspice, cinnamon, and cloves scent the cupboards. A refrigerator the size of a bedroom closet holds what looks like the produce section of the supermarket. And lots and lots of soft drinks and beer.

Cabinets burst with appliances of all kinds: food processors, blenders, mixers, electric knives. Cooking vessels from everywhere can be found: woks, bamboo steamers, pressure cookers, slow cookers, fondue pots and chafing dishes. There's usually an array of cutlery, including French and Chinese, and what could be surgical instruments. And there are also stacks of cookery books of culinary styles the world over.

Mixing it up in a Californian kitchen

Jazzing it up

It is doubtful that all of this abundance gets used on a regular basis. Californians like to keep up and keep aware. They'll rush off in any direction to follow something new. They'll study and practice and learn. And they'll keep a few things close at hand and bring others out just for special occasions or for when they're bored.

Home-Prepared Foods

So what do Golden Staters eat at home? All the usual suspects found in kitchens all over America, and then some. Of course meatloaf and pot roast are family standards, as are fried chicken with cream gravy and buttermilk biscuits; waffles and pancakes; soups and sandwiches; and pizza. And while they don't like to admit to it, they love Pop-Tarts, Top Ramen, TV dinners and Spam. Especially Spam.

The home kitchen reveals a curious dichotomy in the Californian soul. Californians are among those blessed people of the Earth who live to eat rather than eat to live. Their better restaurants are among the best in the world, and they are keenly aware of this and revel in it. Even their middling restaurants are better than most, so they say (and not without cause). But do not think that they are less attracted to junk food than any other group of Americans. (Even the author of this book eats Spam, and if you wanna fight about it just say so!) For all the wonderful bread available in California, the home kitchen is likely to include that lightweight stuff that all Americans dose with peanut butter and jelly. While the Golden State is up to its eyeballs in world-class cheeses, the home kitchen's fridge is likely to hold individually wrapped Kraft American Singles (what young children often refer to as "orange cheese"). Industrial hot dogs nestle next to organic venison sausages; nonfat pasteurized cow's milk from a mega-dairy sits side-by-side with organic raw goat's milk yogurt; and vine-ripened heirloom tomatoes share shelf space with Twinkies. And mere hours before they uncork that premium varietal wine from a cult winemaker, a Golden Stater might well have been enjoying a caffeine-free Diet Cherry Coke, or a pitcher of Kool-Aid. We ascribe no meaning to this culinary dichotomy, for we find none. Please pass the Spam.

There are certain things, though, that are common to the Californian home kitchen, and that are not looked down upon. Avocados are everywhere, and find their way into salads, sandwiches, soups, and guacamole (see p51). Artichokes are almost required by law. The most common way to prepare them is to simmer them in water and dress with mayo. But they are also deep-fried, rendered into soup, baked into breads, or hollowed out and stuffed with crab. Oranges? You want oranges? They got oranges! They've also got sweetcorn, sweet potatoes, sweetbreads; all the leafy greens you've ever heard of and some you haven't; an astounding range of mushrooms; asparagus (skinny, which is steamed, and fat, which is grilled); sausages made from turkey, chicken, venison, pork, sea scallops, or tofu; and Spam.

Home-Cooked Meals

Most of California's residents were born elsewhere or are close descendants of those born elsewhere. Many dishes found on Californian dinner tables are influenced by the various cultures that have come together to form something uniquely Californian – tacos and chop suey are just two dishes that mean "home" to most Californians.

Taco

The taco is ubiquitous. In its Mexican homeland this is simple nosh: a small, soft corn tortilla made of ground corn and water, folded in half and filled with bits of fried meat or fish, some shredded sweet cabbage, and a simple dressing or salsa. One might think of it as a Mexican roulade. The word taco itself means cylinder, plug, or dowel. A champion billiard shooter's cue is sometimes referred to as a *taco de oro*, or golden stick. In Cal-Mex tradition, however, nothing is as the original. A Californian taco is usually a specially made, large, prefolded, crisp tortilla (known as a taco shell) looking somewhat like a huge, bent corn chip. It is filled with fried ground beef, shredded cheddar cheese and lettuce, diced tomato, and sour cream. No Mexican would recognize it. Busy parents find this the perfect meal at home. Mom or Dad can lay out the various ingredients on a single platter, and let the kids assemble their own as they like. No crockery or flatware is required. Many Californians can't live meaningful lives without the taco. Supermarkets sell the makings, fast fooderies flog it to the hurried, and the

Lunch at home in California

careful and constant make their own at home from scratch and are the envy of their neighbors. If you are in the deep south of the state you will come across the more traditional variety. They are quite often made with fried fish, and are magic in your mouth. You may also find what are called "fish tacos" in the north, but they are base impostors, having nothing of the flavor or richness of the real deal.

Chop Suey

We can't really call this dish Chinese, but neither is it western; and it's not fusion, not even close. It would seem to be in a class by itself. At most we can call it Chinese-inspired. It is a dish of overcooked vegetables done in a wok. It may also incorporate the remains of last night's chicken breast or suggestions of tomorrow's beef. It's one of those dishes that is more a concept than a recipe, but it always includes celery, onion, thin noodles, and a gloppy sauce. Common additions are sliced water chestnuts, bean sprouts, and bamboo shoots. Infinitesimal amounts of soy sauce finish it off.

Chop suey was, for perhaps a century, a constant of the Californian culinary landscape. It was on the menu of every typical Chinese restaurant, with at least one patron in a party of four always taking refuge in the security of chop suey, knowing it would not challenge their palate. Tinned versions abounded on supermarket shelves. Recipes appeared in ladies' magazines. "As American as chop suey" was a popular quip.

Its origin is undocumented, but we know that Chinese laborers on the railroad and in the mines had little access to their traditional sources of supply, and just had to make do with what they had. Celery and onions were easily had locally, and noodles were among the earliest imports, while soy sauce was in short supply. With these and other ingredients available willy-nilly, they did the best they could. Eventually they began to sell their improvisations to American and European miners and adventurers. When asked what it was they often replied *tsa sui* ("a bit of this and that") – or chop suey.

You will rarely find this dish in restaurants anymore. It's now homely fare, although California's restaurant chefs are inclined from time to time to turn their gaze backward and serve up a dish of nostalgia. Not long ago the humble pot roast was commanding high prices in some of the best restaurants. Meat loaf with mashed potatoes and gravy makes an appearance now and then. But for chop suey, you gotta go home.

celebrating
with food

Californians love to party, and you should have no trouble finding
a celebration. And even when the calendar shows no statutory holiday or harvest festival, the smell of barbecue will alert you to the fact
that the Californians are celebrating just another great day in the
Golden State.

Californians celebrate with food in two principal ways. The statutory holidays are occasions for feasting, usually at home. For Thanksgiving Day and Christmas the roast turkey is mandatory. Ham is also popular, as well as pumpkin, corn, and a variety of sweets. Other holidays, such as Independence Day and Labor Day, are most often occasions for backyard barbecues, or for picnics at a ball game, auto race, or other public function.

Independence Day picnic: Got any Spam?

Celebratory Food
Barbecued Food

Californians will use any excuse to barbecue, but holidays make it almost obligatory. Even Thanksgiving Day has become an excuse to barbecue. Yes, they will barbecue the turkey! One of the most commonly asked questions about barbecue is not what it consists of, but from whence the name? Consult an English dictionary and it is likely to say that it comes from the Spanish *barbacoa*. Open a Spanish dictionary and it is likely to say that it is the Hispanicized form of the English "barbecue." Linguists have no definitive answer to this weighty question, but we think the most compelling is that it comes from the same type of source as the word *buccaneer* (a French pirate of the Caribbean). Early French adventurers in North America lived largely on meat. At first it was game, and later cattle as well. They would slaughter a moose, steer, or bullock, mount it on a spit and roast it, whole, from beard to tail – from *barbe à queue*.

A great Californian pastime: the barbecue

In America, the barbecue began in very early colonial-era days on the Atlantic coast, chiefly in the South. In the northeast a seaside version of outdoor cookery called the clambake is practiced, in which shellfish and corn (maize) are cooked in a pit of hot stones. Beef cattle have always been fewer in the northeast, as have sunny days and the kinds of woods favored by barbecue aficionados. The institution of the "barbecue pit" made its way west with the growing nation, and as it penetrated new regions it accommodated itself to local ways and products. In addition to the original Southern style there is the Kansas City style, Texas style, Chicago style (the city of big shoulders not wanting to be left out), and a dozen other lesser-known styles.

The Californian style is distinctive in that it did not make its way gradually west as did the aforementioned styles. It was already there, alive and well, when the 49ers arrived. It had come with the Spanish/Mexican predecessors. It was born of the fiesta, the fandango, and the rodeo. Unlike the Midwestern styles, it does not generally rely on sauce. It's more like the Southern style, which relies on smoke. But in California there is a penchant for marinades, and spice or herb rubs, with less emphasis on smoke.

Until the mid-20th century, the home barbecue was largely the prerogative of the affluent and the rural. Common city dwellers simply lacked the space, equipment, and fuel. There were barbecue restaurants, however. One of the most famous was Chasen's restaurant in Hollywood, which began as a simple barbecue pit on the outskirts of Tinsel Town. Big Stone Lodge in San Diego has been burning since the 1920s, as has Henry's World Famous Hi-Life in San Jose. The latter began as a flophouse for Italian laborers in the orchards of what would become Silicon Valley. It quickly became better known, and well loved, for its brick-oven barbecue. Like many an old barbecue pit, the locals take a proprietary and protective view of it. During disastrous flooding in the late-20th century, legions of neighborhood folk and the San Jose Sharks hockey team spontaneously rushed to the rescue and sandbagged the place. Californians *will* have their barbecue restaurants regardless of Mother Nature's tantrums.

But home barbecue requires that legacy of the ranchos of old California – the patio. After WWII, the boom in the US economy had record numbers of people building and buying houses. And in California, the idea of "house" became inseparable from "patio." At first the patio barbecue was strictly a masculine form of cookery. Men who had previously lived for their cars were now building brick or stone towers of barbecue bastions and accoutering them with a dazzling array of utensils, changeable grills, and cleaning gear; indulging in the endless arguments of charcoal versus wood, and sauce versus no sauce; wearing funny aprons; reading barbecue magazines; and generally enjoying themselves immensely. Being the province of

A Californian indigenous-style barbecue

household Alpha Males, the act of grilling together became a ritual of male bonding. Father taught son the mysteries of marinade, and to know the exact moment to turn each kind of meat. Friends and coworkers grilled together, swilling beer and contemplating the good life. Neighbors competed lustily for titles like Barbecue King of Southeast Central Smallville.

Nowadays even apartment dwellers barbecue, and some are women! Companies like Weber have developed smaller and smaller grilling apparatus, both charcoal and gas fired. Anybody with a square foot of outdoor space can indulge, and Californians will grill literally anything. All kinds of vegetables are staples of the Californian barbecue, with asparagus, sweet peppers, mushrooms, and onions especially popular. Whole heads of garlic, slices of fennel, radicchio, and tomatoes get grilled. We have even seen vegan Californians happily barbecuing tofu (bean curd). About the only thing a Golden Stater won't put on a grill is a raw egg. But you can bet that somewhere one of them is trying. Happy holidays!

Tamale

The most ancient culinary preparation in North America is probably the tamale. In proper Spanish the singular is *tamal*, ta-**mahl**. The plural is *tamales*, ta-**mah**-lays. Most non-Hispanic Californians, however, say tamale, ta-**mah**-lay, for the singular. A cornmeal pocket filled with meat, cheese, or vegetables, wrapped in corn husks and steamed or baked over a fire, it has sustained American peoples for millennia. In Southern California this is soul food, comfort food, and holiday fare. Since Spanish days, people have served tamales for Christmas dinner, birthdays, and other special occasions. In Mexico, the standard filling is pork, maybe chicken, and pieces of black olive. In California, they can not only be filled with all kinds of savories, but also with sweets such as chocolate, fruit preserves, or custard. In Los Angeles, El Cholo Cafe is famous for its green corn tamales, served in late spring/early summer.

Green tamales, El Cholo Cafe

Harvest Festivals

From spring through fall there are seemingly innumerable harvest festivals. They are uproarious, whacky, fun, lighthearted, and full of good things to eat. They will often include a parade of some sort, exhibitions of dance, music, art, or just exhibitionism. And they usually include a beauty contest wherein the winner is proclaimed the queen of whatever crop is being celebrated. Screen siren Marilyn Monroe once reigned as the Artichoke Queen of Castro Valley. There is a carrot queen, a nut queen, and orange, apple, and pear queens. The complete list would be too long to print. And it's not just plant foods that are celebrated either. The Mendocino Crab and Wine Days festival (**W** www.gomendo.com/events) is held in January. But as far as we know they do not nominate a Queen of Crabs.

Gilroy Garlic Festival

From ancient to modern times, garlic has been associated with laborers, soldiers, peasants, and the great unwashed, earning the ire of snobs of every place and time. The Roman writer Horace penned an epigram, "To the garlic eater: May thy mistress refuse to kiss thee!" In Renaissance England, Thomas Nashe complained that garlic produced drowsiness, thirst, and bad breath, writing that it "causeth a man to winke, drinke, and stinke!" Though the prophet Mohammed prescribed it for bites and stings, he did not like the smell, and pious Muslims still refrain from eating it before going to mosque, so as not to offend.

Come to Gilroy and take the air

And there, in a nutshell, is the age-old controversy over garlic: people with sissy noses think it stinks. People of pretentious proboscis have looked down their sniveling sniffers at it since Noah was a cabin boy. In fairness to the fancy and faint, we should point out that before very recent times garlic was eaten raw as often as cooked, as were radishes and scallions (spring onions).

But let the highborn, the prissy, and the snob go their bland and lightly seasoned ways. All who love the taste and smell, come to California and follow your noses to the little town of Gilroy, where the Garlic Festival draws over 150,000 lovers of the pungent lily. People come, literally, by the trainload to feast on garlic-laden food, to commune with other alliophiles, and to "take the Gilroy air." It is perhaps the most famous and best-attended harvest festival in California.

Preparing for the hungry hordes at the Gilroy Garlic Festival

Cooking contests are a favorite part of the garlic festival

CELEBRATING

For all its similarities to a Kansas corn fest or a Midwest wheat fair, the Garlic Festival is unique, situated in a vast open field rather than the county fairgrounds. All revelers are keenly aware that huge numbers of people wouldn't come within 30 smelly miles of Gilroy if they could avoid it, and they find that delightfully funny. The collective congregation is a joyous rebuke to every gastronomic snob that praised a steamed filet of sole with parsley, but choked on the aroma of the sacred bulb.

Thousands attend the Gilroy Garlic Festival each year

And at the same time, all in attendance have a common love and respect for garlic. The people drape themselves with braids of garlic and festoon their hats with its bulbs. Perfect strangers swap recipes and garlicky tales, and toast each other with garlic wine. The cooks on Gourmet Alley serve up enough garlic fare to go through eight tons of the stinking rose (the presence of numerous Mexican and Thai cooks ensures a lot of chile being used as well). "How does it taste?" is a frequent question asked along that long row of food stalls. "Great! But it could use more garlic," is the common answer. Herbalists, doctors and medical researchers disseminate their findings on the healthful uses of garlic. And over $3,000,000 of the festival's proceeds have gone to worthy causes.

The Gilroy Garlic Festival is held annually, during the last weekend in July. For more information contact Gilroy Garlic Festival Association Inc.; PO Box 2311, 7473 Monterey St, Gilroy CA 95021, ☎ 408-842-1625.

CALIFORNIA CULINARY COUNCILOR

California has an embarrassment of riches in its demimonde of gastronomy. So many fine restaurants, literally thousands, and no time for them all. How to choose that special place to celebrate Valentine's Day? I have a secret method. And it works 100% of the time. It's very scientific. And just 'cause I like the cut of your jib I'm gonna explain it to ya. So when you see me on the street, you remember to say thanks. See?

Now, everybody who lives or works in the Golden State already knows the restaurant you want to find. It might be expensive or cheap, this place you want. Could be in the local Little Italy, or Koreatown, up the avenues, or down some foggy alley. It might be simple Mexican, snooty French, inscrutable Chinese. As yet, you don't know. The one thing you do know is that it's not some overly popular, oh-so-trendy joint with a celeb chef who draws in the jaded herd and those who wanna-be. No, this place you're looking for, whatever its kind, is the best of its kind.

And so you have to ask this one simple question, of your One Who Knows. You ask a business district suit, knowing you'll get one answer. You ask a cab driver, knowing you'll get another. You ask a soccer mom, a journalist, a bike messenger, a cop, or a crook. You ask any class of person this one question: "Where would you go if you wanted to propose marriage?" I haven't once gotten bad advice.

regional
variations

It's the second-largest of the 48 contiguous states, the most popu-
lous of the 50, and possessed of an economy larger than that of
France. But as numerous and diverse as Californians are, they show
little regional difference. At least as far we can see on a map. But
California is also a state of mind, and that has its geography, too.

Coit tower in San Francisco

It's fairly simple to divide California geographically, culturally, and politically. A simple north-south split raises few objections. A former governor of California once suggested the dividing line be drawn from a spot on Highway 99 in Fresno County where a palm tree sidles up north-south with a pine tree. "Draw the line where the palm tree meets the pine," said he. But California isn't just a portion of the map. It is also the realm of imagination, of human invention, of fiction so true it must be thought of as real. And so two other territories emerge. Not as regions but as dimensions, as states of mind, as perceived experience. They are La Frontera and the open road.

REGIONS

Oregon

Idaho

USA

Nevada

San Francisco

California

Utah

Pacific
Ocean

Los Angeles

Arizona

MEXICO

NorCal
SoCal

Northern California

The history of the American state of California begins in the north, and pretty much stays there until the rise of Hollywood in the 1920s. Northerners are very conscious of that, and like to see themselves as keepers of the hearth flame. The state's political capital is the northern city of Sacramento, just downstream from where gold was first discovered at Sutter's Mill on the Sacramento River. Gold Rush gastronomy is enshrined in such San Francisco places as Tadich Grill, established in 1849 and still operated by the same family. You can taste history at Jack's, established in 1864, which specialized back then in locally caught jackrabbit. The nation's oldest Italian restaurant, Fior D'Italia, started in 1886 at 504 Broadway. In 1954 it moved to larger premises around the corner and the old space was taken over by Enrico Banducci. Operating as a coffeehouse, Enrico's became a favorite haunt of writers of the Beat Generation. Jack Kerouac wrote much of his work there. It's a lot fancier these days, but is still serving up history. And even in fiction, detective Sam Spade regularly patronizes John's Grill on Ellis Street (established in 1903). The state's oldest saloon (established in 1861) is called, fittingly, The Saloon, and is on Grant Street. Jack London's favorite resort is across the bay in Oakland, Heinold's First and Last Chance Saloon.

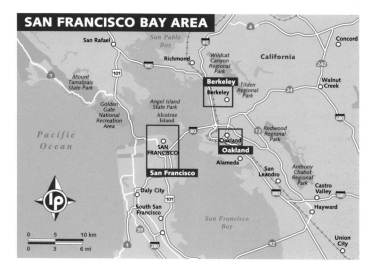

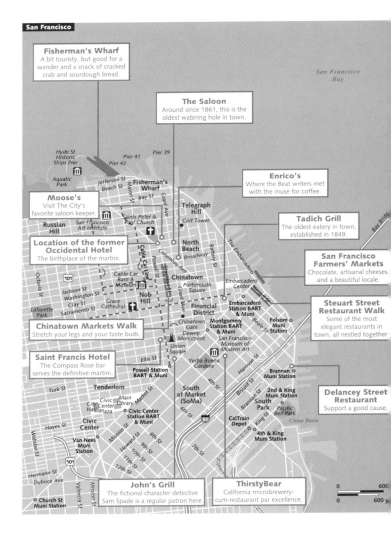

San Francisco

Fisherman's Wharf
A bit touristy, but good for a wander and a snack of cracked crab and sourdough bread.

The Saloon
Around since 1861, this is the oldest watering hole in town.

San Francisco Bay

Enrico's
Where the Beat writers met with the muse for coffee.

Hyde St Historic Ships Pier

Pier 41   Pier 39
Pier 43

Aquatic Park

Jefferson St   Fisherman's
Beach St   Wharf

Moose's
Visit The City's favorite saloon keeper.

Mason St   Bay St

Grant Ave

Telegraph Hill

Coit Tower

Tadich Grill
The oldest eatery in town, established in 1849.

Bay Bridge

Russian Hill   San Francisco Art Institute

Saints Peter & Paul Church

Location of the former Occidental Hotel
The birthplace of the martini.

Columbus Ave

North Beach
Broadway

Battery St

The Embarcadero

San Francisco Farmers' Markets
Chocolate, artisanal cheeses and a beautiful locale.

Octavia St

101

Cable Car Barn & Museum

Jackson St
Washington St
Clay St
Sacramento St

Cable Car Line

Powell St

Grace Cathedral

Nob Hill

Chinatown

Portsmouth Square

Grant Ave

Embarcadero Center

Steuart Street Restaurant Walk
Some of the most elegant restaurants in town, all nestled together

Lafayette Park

Chinatown Markets Walk
Stretch your legs and your taste buds.

Chinatown Gate   Montgomery
Dewey   Station BART
Monument   & Muni

Financial District

Embarcadero Station BART & Muni

Folsom
St Station

Saint Francis Hotel
The Compass Rose bar serves the definitive martini.

Ellis St

Powell Station BART & Muni

Union Square

San Francisco Museum of Modern Art

Yerba Buena Gardens

Harrison St

Brannan St

Brannan Muni Station

Delancey Street Restaurant
Support a good cause.

Turk St

Tenderloin

Main Library

City Center
Hall Plaza

Civic Center Station BART & Muni

Civic Center

Market St

South of Market (SoMa)

4th St

Bryant St

2nd & King
Muni Station

South Park   Pacific
Bell Park

Hayes St

Van Ness Muni Station

Mission St   Howard St

6th St

40

CalTrain Depot

7th St

King St

China Basin

4th & King Muni Station

Webster St

101

8th St
9th St
10th St
11th St
12th St

Hermann St
Duboce Ave

Valencia St

Mission St

Church St
Muni Station

John's Grill
The fictional character detective Sam Spade is a regular patron here.

ThirstyBear
California microbrewery-cum-restaurant par excellence.

0   600
0   600 y

keley

Solano Avenue Restaurant Walk
"hidden" strip of fine restaurants, nown only to the locals. And you.

Martin Luther King Middle School
Home campus of the Edible Schoolyard.

Peet's Coffee & Tea
The starting point of the Californian coffee revolution.

Acme Bakery
he starting point of California's artisanal bakery movement.

Chez Panisse
Where California Cuisine was born.

4th Street Restaurant Walk
This restored industrial area has some of the best-loved eateries in town.

Gourmet Ghetto
A fine dining and produce mecca.

800 m
800 yd

Indian Rock Park
The Alameda
Solano Ave
Fleming Point
Golden Gate Fields (Race Track)
Codornices Creek
Gilman St
Hopkins St
Rose St
Live Oak Park
Codornices Park
La Loma Park
Cedar St
Virginia St
Hearst St
North Berkeley BART Station
Ohlone Park
University Ave
ML King Jr Civic Center Park & Plaza
Addison St
123
Allston Way
Bancroft Way
Dwight Way
Parker St
Derby St
Cesar E Chavez Park
Marina Blvd
Berkeley Marina
San Francisco Bay
Shorebird Park
Berkeley Pier
Aquatic Park
San Pablo Park
Eastshore Fwy
80
580
4th St
6th St
8th St
10th St
Sacramento St
ML King Jr Way
Milvia St
Shattuck Ave
Oxford St
Hearst Ave
University of California, Berkeley
Memorial Stadium
Berkeley BART Station
Bancroft Way
Channing Way
Telegraph Ave
College Ave
San Pablo Ave
Acton St

REGIONAL VARIATIONS

kland

Carrara's
The ultimate car café.

Jack London Square
Restaurants and bars, ncluding Jack's fave – Heinold's First and Last Chance Saloon.

26th St
25th St
27th St
W Grand Ave
Linden St
Myrtle St
Filbert St
Market St
Castro St
Brush St
16th St
14th St
20th St
Telegraph Ave
23rd St
Grand Ave
22nd St
21st St
19th St BART Station
Broadway
Harrison St
Bay Place
Bellevue Ave
Lakeside Ave
Van Buren Ave
Grand Ave
Lakeshore Ave
Hanover Ave
Santa Clara Ave
Grand Ave
580
Perkins St
San Pablo Ave
Clay St
17th St
Webster St
15th St
Harrison St
13th St
Snow Park
Camron-Stanford House
Lake Merritt
4th Ave
7th Ave
8th Ave
3rd Ave
Park Blvd
5th Ave
Jack London Square
City Center
Oakland Convention Centre
12th St/City Center BART Station
8th St
6th St
4th St
3rd St
2nd St
Franklin St
Oakland Museum of California
Chinatown
Lake Merritt BART Station
Peralta Park
Laney College
Channel Park
6th St
7th St
1st Ave
2nd Ave
Foothill Blvd
International Blvd
E 12th St
E 15th St
E 11th St
E 10th St
Amtrak Station
Oakland Inner Harbor
Jack London Museum

500 m
500 yd

Most of the food and recipes for which California is known were created or popularized in the north, such as chop suey, cioppino, the martini, Irish coffee, zinfandel wine, and the It's It ice-cream sandwich. The famous sourdough bread marks its commercial beginning when Isidore Boudin opened his bakery in San Francisco in 1849. This is the stuff that travelers buy at the airport to take home to their less fortunate. Oakland's Frank Epperson invented the Popsicle in 1905. Santa Rosa's Luther Burbank developed the nectarine, and scores of other fruits and vegetables that are now taken for granted. In 1939 Johnny Kan of San Francisco started Chinese Kitchen, the first authentic Chinese delivery service in the US. And in 1944 "Trader Vic" Bergeron invented the mai tai cocktail, thus providing humanity with a perfect excuse to buy and drink rum.

> East is east and west is San Francisco ... Californians are a race of people; they are not merely inhabitants of a state.
>
> *O. Henry (William Sydney Porter), short-story writer, 1910*

DON'T MISS

- A cooking lesson at the CIA
- A ceremonial martini at the Compass Rose bar
- A pilgrimage to Chez Panisse (make reservations)
- Dungeness crab, especially in a bowl of cioppino
- Garlic in Gilroy if you're there in July

Northern Californians have a greater awareness of wine than their southern counterparts, but that should be no surprise, as wine is one of the major northern crops. Wine would be taken for granted were it not so revered. Important winemakers, great and small, are regional celebrities. On the other hand, it could be argued that southerners have a greater awareness of cocktails. Well, they drink more of them. Other important northern crops include apples of many varieties, cherries, strawberries, pears, and rice. Cattle are also raised here, for meat as well as for dairy products. And then there is the wonderful Northern Californian seafood (see Sand Dabs, p146).

While Northern California has a rich Gold Rush history, it is also, thanks to the sometimes quiet, sometimes tumultuous university town of Berkeley, the birthplace of California Cuisine. Many restaurants follow the example of Chez Panisse (see p16) and have dedicated growers who provide the restaurant's more-important ingredients. Some take it even further and grow their own. In the far northern town of Eureka, luxurious Carter House grows most of its own herbs and vegetables within sight of the dining room. In San Francisco the North Beach Restaurant grows grapes and makes its own wine, and cures its own prosciutto. While the vineyards are in Napa, the hams are cured hanging from the ceiling in the restaurant's basement, which doubles as a function room for private banquets or overflowing crowds on busy nights. Dining under the hanging hams is delicious. So are the hams!

Classics of the North
Hangtown Fry

Along with Levi's jeans, redwood hot tubs, and the martini, hangtown fry is one of the few things that actually originated in California. Back in the glory days of the Gold Rush, the little town of Placerville was like so many others in the Sierra foothills of the "gold country." Garden-variety shootings, knifings, and beatings competed desperately for newspaper space with the richer and more lurid villainies of which humanity is capable. The sheriff alone was not up to the task of asserting the writ of the government. Vigilante law, where the local citizenry tried, condemned, and hanged felons with breathtaking efficiency, came to prevail. So, Placerville came to be called Hangtown. Today Placerville is perfectly safe to visit, and though the "vigilance committee" no longer convenes, you should still think twice about knifing anyone while there.

You should, however, think about enjoying this little town's chief contribution to human happiness. (This is assuming the hanging of criminals is not a chief source of happiness for you. For that you need another book.) During the Gold Rush, hundreds of thousands of men ran off to find the "gold in them thar hills," only to find failure. Merely a handful struck it rich in the goldfields. But many others profited well, by supplying the hopeful with necessities and luxuries. Levi Strauss, with his famous riveted trousers, is the best-known example. But restaurant owners and grocers also did well. Not to mention saloon keepers, dance-hall girls, and courtesans. (Again, that's another book.)

Hangtown Fry

This recipe has been supplied courtesy of the Pasadena Junior League's *California Cookbook*.

Ingredients

Omelet Mix

6	eggs
¼ cup (60mL)	heavy (whipping) cream
¼ cup	parsley, chopped
¼ cup	parmesan cheese, grated
	salt & pepper

Oysters

6–8	oysters, shucked and rinsed
2	eggs, beaten
10–12	soda crackers, crushed into crumbs

Garnish

½ lb (225g)	bacon
2	sprigs parsley

In a mixing bowl beat the 6 eggs with the cream, chopped parsley, and cheese, and then season with the salt and pepper.

In a large greased skillet (frypan), fry the bacon until crisp and then set aside. Remove all but about 6 tablespoons of grease from the skillet. Dip the oysters in the 2 beaten eggs, then roll in the cracker crumbs. Fry them in the bacon grease over medium heat, for about one minute each side.

Pour the omelet mixture over the oysters in the skillet, reducing the heat to low. Lift the oysters so the mixture surrounds them. Cook until the eggs are semi-firm but still moist, then place the skillet under a broiler (griller) to brown the omelet lightly.

Slide the omelet from the skillet onto a heated platter, and serve garnished with the bacon strips and sprigs of parsley.

Serves 6

When our burly goldseeker came down from the mount with his hard-earned "poke" full of nuggets or dust, he was determined to have the best and dearest the wide-open frontier town could offer. In those days oysters were considered the height of culinaria, and were far away on the coast. Chickens and pigs were also held in high esteem. Hence, to the goldseekers, oysters, eggs, and bacon were the gastronomic mother lode that awaited the successful digger.

Hangtown Fry, Tadich Grill, San Francisco

Sand Dabs

These delicate morsels are also known as the Left Eyed Flounder of the Left Coast, because both the fish's eyes are situated on the left side, and because New Yorkers refer to California as the "Left Coast." This makes sense if you look at the map or spin a globe. When the weather is fine the smaller craft launch from Half Moon Bay and Bodega Bay and regularly bring back hauls of California's favorite bottom-dweller, *Citharichthys sordidus*. On average they weigh a mere quarter-pound. One sand dab makes an appetizer, though they are seldom served as such. Traditionally two or three of them make a lunch, but rarely a dinner. These are a midday meal, served with sourdough bread, butter, and a crisp white wine, cold beer, or iced tea. They are almost always prepared meunière-style – breaded, fried in butter, and tarted up with a bit of lemon. Nothing that will interfere with their native delicate taste and aroma. They are usually brought to you, one atop the other, on a simple

Faces of Gastronomy – THE SALOON LORD

Tendrils of fog are gently making their nightly probe into the North Beach neighborhood of San Francisco. Pedestrians are pulling on gloves and buttoning up their collars. And yet in the golden light of Moose's Restaurant, on Washington Square, it couldn't be more comfy and cozy. The jazz trio is playing, martinis are shaking, duck breasts are searing, salads of microgreens (see the boxed text Faces of Gastronomy – Mr. Greens, p154) and heirloom tomatoes are tossing, and the nightly party is getting underway. San Francisco's own favorite host, Ed Moose, is at the center of it. Ed is restaurateur and saloon keeper to the high and mighty, and to the average Joe, and he revels in it.

Ed and his wife, Mary Etta, came to public attention in the 1970s when they were proprietors of the nearby Washington Square Bar & Grill (known affectionately as the WashBag). There journalists and politicos of both high and low repute rubbed elbows, drank, swapped stories, told whoppers, and ate meat and potatoes and a bit of Italian fare. Ed and Mary Etta later sold the WashBag, and eventually opened the eponymous restaurant on the opposite side of the square. Now Ed presides, Mary Etta tinkers with recipes (her chile con carne is legendary), and chef Jason Miller sends wonderful things out from the kitchen. Restaurant critics often refer to Moose's as a Californian-style brassiere, but Ed likes to call it "my saloon."

In our not-so-humble opinion, Moose's captures the spirit of both Gold Rush and modern California better than any other joint in the whole Golden State. That means frontier egalitarianism coupled with the best of food, drink, and music. It means a place where, as Ed says, "You can white plate, napped with a sauce of pan drippings, and garnished with a wedge of lemon and sprig of parsley. Anything more is thought to be pretentious or, worse, "Right Coast." They will be golden brown and crisp, redolent of the sea, and eager to leap into your mouth and commend themselves to your body. They are California making love to your mouth. Their taste says "Welcome to the Golden State, and bon appetite."

Do not ask for them to be filleted. They are too small, and the bones contribute flavor during cooking. You may ask for them cleaned and beheaded, and such will you get. But aficionados (and virtually everyone on the north coast is an aficionado) take them just as nature and Neptune made them: head, tail, guts, and all. They're quite salubrious as such, and tastier, too. You are not expected to eat the viscera. Though you may, if you are Greek or Chinese, feel free to suck the flesh from the head. We always claim to be Greek or Chinese.

REGIONAL VARIATIONS

have a meal for $10, or max out your gold card and be satisfied either way." You can nurse your suds at the bar while watching a ball game, or you might find yourself seated next to Hizzonor da Mayor as you chew through a grass-fed beefsteak or a vegetarian risotto. A local film star might flip coins with you for a drink. No one is above another, and all are on a high plane.

Ed and Mary Etta are typical Gold Rush Californians, in that they came from somewhere else. They moved from Missouri, where Ed was a sports writer and Mary Etta ran a nightclub. But the lure of the Golden State brought them west to stay. And in so doing

Ed Moose at Moose's Restaurant

they have become stewards of certain Californian cultural treasures, not the least of which is something very good to eat. This is cioppino, something that can only be had in Northern California, and nowhere else on the great gastronomical globe, for it relies on strictly local ingredients, and they don't travel well.

Cioppino

When the native Dungeness crabs are being harvested you must dive into a bowl of cioppino (cho-peen-oh), a tomato-based seafood dish that the late, revered food writer Roy Andres DeGroot described as, "the finest regional dish in America." Developed over decades by fishermen hailing from Sicily, Portugal, and home waters, it's an improvisational recipe and is open to argument. Like the population of the state, its ribbons of contribution are numerous and disparate. But all agree on the basic approach, and that it must contain the distinctive local crab and rockfish. The dish is bold yet subtle, earthy, and refined – the very reflection of Northern California in a soup bowl. It screams for your attention while seducing you slyly.

It was famous at the WashBag. It is now famous at Moose's (see the boxed text Faces of Gastronomy – The Saloon Lord, p146). It was once a common dish and famous all over. But due to smaller harvests you now must travel to find it. So travel, and find it! If you can't get yourself to Moose's, or can't find it otherwise, they'd still like for you to taste this dish. So they have provided the recipe, just as it is done by chef Jason Miller.

Cioppino ingredients ready to go

Cioppino

Ingredients

2	live Dungeness crabs
3 tbs	oil
4	cloves garlic, minced
2	leeks (white part only), finely chopped
1/2	green pepper (capsicum), minced
12	two-inch chunks of Californian ling cod, lightly salted
12	live manila clams in shell, scrubbed clean
12	large whole shrimp
6 fl oz (175mL)	dry white wine
6 fl oz (175mL)	rich fish stock
2 cups	ripe tomatoes, peeled, seeded, and chopped
1/2 tsp	hot red pepper, dried and crushed
	salt & pepper

Lay the crabs on their backs and, with one whack of a sharp cleaver, bisect them from head to tail. Remove the back shells and all grey fibrous matter. Separate the claws and legs, and lightly crack the shells. In a large pot, heat the oil over a low flame. Sauté the garlic, leeks, and green pepper until tender. Raise the heat to medium and add the crab sections, sautéeing until they begin to color. Add the ling cod (which, as it disintegrates, it will give the dish its characteristic gelatinous consistency) and the remaining ingredients and cook at medium heat for 5 minutes.
    Serves 6

Southern California

Perhaps the most interesting thing about California's regional variations is the fierce rivalry the north (mostly San Francisco) feels toward the south (Los Angeles). While this rivalry is lusty, vigorous, and full of invective and territorial particularism, SoCal (Southern California) is largely unaware of it. Venerable SF is always ready to remind upstart LA of who is the senior city. A popular cry is "SF eats LA's lunch!"

Much of Southern California's gastronomy is centered on Mexican-inspired Cal-Mex, which could be thought of as a subset of Southwestern cookery. The cookery of the American Southwest, of which California is a part, is a more varied practice than most people, even Southwesterners, are aware. But if we can distill the various tributaries of this culinary pool into one essence, it would be chile salsa. Not a particular chile salsa, but chile salsa as a concept, an idea, as a balance of salt, sweet, sour, and hot that enhances the flavor of blander foods such as corn and beans while stimulating the gastric juices and pleasing the senses. It can be made from chiles that are green or red, fresh or dry, smoked, roasted, fried, steamed, chopped, sliced, or puréed. Some are smooth and pourable. Some are full of chunky vegetables, even fruits, and are satisfying to eat with a spoon right from the jar. You will never taste them all, but it's fun to try.

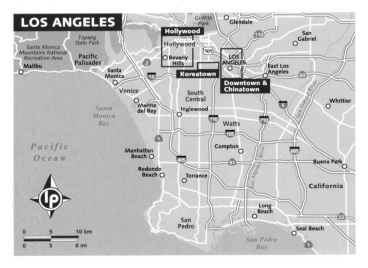

A popular conception of Southern California is of Hollywood, tanning salons, plastic surgery, surfing, and strip malls. And all of those images are valid. As are the panache of Wolfgang Puck, the subtle artistry of Robert Gadsby (see the boxed text Faces of Gastronomy – Mr. Greens, p154), and the conspicuous consumption of Palm Springs. SoCal is a wonderful place to eat – you'll find some the best food in the world here. Especially if you are looking for Korean, Japanese, Indian, or other Asian fare. The greater LA area probably has more gastronomic diversity than any other place on Earth. People in New York might argue but, hey, what's life without a little cussin' and discussin'? What none should deny, though, is that this region is one of the best places to find what folk call "comfort food" (for an example see French-dip Sandwich, p158). This is stuff that is big in the mouth, robustly flavored but not too heavily spiced, rich, plentiful, and with potatoes on the side. Before that puckish Wolfie arrived on the scene, the most famous restaurants in Hollywood were Chasen's with its chile, the Brown Derby with its Cobb salad, and Musso & Frank Grill's, with a lengthy menu of meat and potatoes dishes. The former two are no more, but you may still put on the feedbag at M&Fs in downtown Hollywood. And let us not fail to mention El Cholo Cafe. Established in 1927, El Cholo Cafe is widely held to be the original Cal-Mex restaurant. Try the green-corn tamales (see Tamale, p132).

REGIONAL VARIATIONS

El Cholo Cafe, Los Angeles

REGIONAL VARIATIONS

Hollywood

Hollywood & Highland
Glitz, glamour, and good eats, all in a modern shopping complex.

Laurel Canyon

Bristol Farms Market
Retaining a small corner of the famous Chasen's restaurant, and still serving Chasen's chile con carne.

Runyon Canyon Park

Wattles Garden Park

Scenic Gardens

Hollywood Bowl

Hollywood Franklin Ave

Hollywood/ Highland

Hollywood Blvd

Hawthorn Ave

W Sunset Blvd

Hollywood

Delongpre Park

William S Hart Park

N Crescent Heights Blvd

N Fairfax Ave

Fountain Ave

Santa Monica Blvd

Warner Hollywood Studios

N Gardner St

Musso & Frank Grill
Hollywood comfort food.

W Sunset Blvd

Willoughby St

West Hollywood

Santa Monica Blvd

Pacific Design Center

N La Cienega Blvd

Clinton St

Melrose Ave

Poinsettia Recreation Center

N La Brea Ave

S Highland Ave

Melrose/ La Brea

Highland Ave

The Wils Country C

Beverly Gardens Park

N Beverly Blvd

S Doheny Drive

Beverly Center District

Oakwood Ave

Rosewood Ave

Fairfax District

Cedars-Sinai Medical Center

Beverly Center

S Robertson Blvd

Beverly Blvd

Beverly Hills

Burton Way

San Vicente Blvd

Colgate Ave

CBS Television City

Pan Pacific Park

LA's Farmers' Market
The grandest of all.

W 3rd St

Wilshire Blvd

Four Seasons Hotel
Drink with the stars in the bar.

S Fairfax Ave

Miracle Mile District

Hancock Park

W 4th St

Mid-City

W 6th St

LA County Museum of Art

Page Museum at La Brea Discoveries

Wilshire Blvd

LA Restaurant Walk
One of the few places in LA where you don't need to drive.

Craft & Folk Art Museum

W 8th St

W 9th St

0   80

0   800

W Olympic Blvd

Whitworth Ave

Koreatown

W 9th St

James M Woods St

Koreatown Plaza

San Marino St

S Western Ave

Ardmore Park

W Olympic Blvd

Fedora St

S Berendo St

S Vermont Ave

S Westmoreland Ave

S Park View St

Hoover St

W 11th St

Country Club Dr

El Cholo Cafe
Classic margaritas, legendary green corn tamales.

W 12th St

S Alvarado St

W 12th St

S Gramercy Pl

Manhattan Pl

W Pico Blvd

St Sophia Cathedral

W Pico Blvd

W 15th St

Normandie Park

0   60

Venice Blvd

0   600

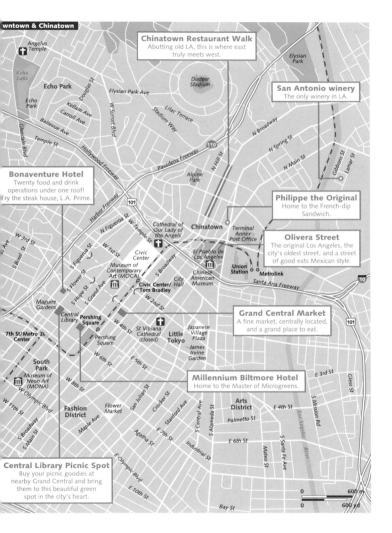

wntown & Chinatown

Angelus Temple

Echo Lake

Echo Park

Echo Park

Douglas St

Kellam Ave

Carroll Ave

Bellevue Ave

Temple St

Glendale Blvd

W Sunset Blvd

Elysian Park Ave

Lilac Terrace

Stadium Way

Dodger Stadium

Elysian Park

Chinatown Restaurant Walk
Abutting old LA, this is where east truly meets west.

San Antonio winery
The only winery in LA.

Hollywood Freeway

Pasadena Freeway

110

N Hill St

N Broadway

N Spring St

N Main St

Gibbons St

Lamar St

Harbor Freeway

101

Alpine Park

Bonaventure Hotel
Twenty food and drink operations under one roof!
Try the steak house, L.A. Prime.

N Figueroa St

W Temple St

Cathedral of Our Lady of the Angels

Chinatown

Terminal Annex Post Office

Philippe the Original
Home to the French-dip Sandwich.

W 3rd St

S Bixel St

S Ave

S Figueroa St

W 1st St

S Flower St

S Hope St

S Grand Ave

W Broadway

Civic Center

Museum of Contemporary Art (MOCA)

City Hall

Civic Center/ Tom Bradley

El Pueblo de Los Angeles

Chinese American Museum

Union Station

Metrolink

Olivera Street
The original Los Angeles, the city's oldest street, and a street of good eats Mexican style.

Santa Ana Freeway

10

Maguire Gardens

Central Library

Pershing Square

W 4th St

Pershing Square

W 2nd St

St Vibiana Cathedral (closed)

Little Tokyo

Japanese Village Plaza

James Irvine Garden

Grand Central Market
A fine market, centrally located, and a grand place to eat.

E 3rd St

101

Gless St

7th St/Metro Center

South Park

Museum of Neon Art (MONA)

W 8th St

W 5th St

E 5th St

W 6th St

Millennium Biltmore Hotel
Home to the Master of Microgreens.

E 3rd St

E 4th St

Arts District

Palmetto St

E Mission Rd

Los Angeles River

W Olympic Blvd

W 11th St

S Broadway

S Main St

Fashion District

Flower Market

Maple Ave

San Julian St

Crocker St

Stanford Ave

Agatha St

E 7th St

Industrial St

S Central Ave

S Alameda St

E 6th St

Mateo St

S Santa Fe Ave

S Santa Fe Ave

Central Library Picnic Spot
Buy your picnic goodies at nearby Grand Central and bring them to this beautiful green spot in the city's heart.

E Olympic Blvd

E 10th St

Bay St

0   600 m
0   600 yd

REGIONAL VARIATIONS

Robert Gadsby pores over his raw materials like a jeweler sorting and grading diamonds. As he utters their names he seems to be addressing them, affectionately. The roll sounds downright poetic – shiro, popcorn sprout, tatsoi, mizuna, peppercress. He can hold them all in his two hands, for these are "microgreens." These are greens that exist naturally as small greens, have been created as "micro" versions of ordinary-sized plants, or are ordinary plants picked young.

Gadsby is the Executive Chef of the famous Millennium Biltmore Hotel (birthplace of the Academy Awards) in Los Angeles. Here he has long practiced a culinary art that has started catching on all over California, and now even beyond.

Robert Gadsby with microgreens grower Sean, Biltmore Hotel

> I was inspired at first by my experience working in Japan. There the small and exquisite are highly prized, as well as balance between the concepts of earth, sea, and sky. In this view of culinary cosmology microgreens represent sky.

These are words from a man who trained in France and Italy as a classic European chef. How typically Californian, to bring together such disparate threads of contribution and tie them together into a beautiful bow. "Magenta spinach, oba, microchrysanthemum, microfennel," he continues as he cuts leaves from living plants growing in little trays in the kitchen. In mere minutes they will be a composition of salad on a plate before some amazed diner.

> I cook with them also, but only very gently and quickly. They mustn't lose their color or texture. Some of them are naturally small, some are simply harvested young. A lot of Californian chefs are using them now. I'm originally from London and I know that a number of chefs there are importing the little darlings from here in California. And through London they're making their way to Germany. Who knows how far they'll go. We seem to have started a worldwide trend. But then that's what California does best.

However, southerners, like their northern counterparts, are also always on the prowl for more-sophisticated eats. But they do tend to eat differently. While all Californians love salad, southerners love it even more and often make a dinner of it. If the menu shows a salad costing more than a few dollars it's probably meant to be a meal, not a starter. Southerners also tip a little more, with 20% being the standard. While northerners will make an evening of dinner, and so tend to start relatively late, southerners, especially in LA, start early and have dinner rather as an hors d'oeuvre to the whole of an evening. The southland has a richer nightlife of theater, concerts, exhibitions, and events to see and be seen in. It's common, upon being seated in the restaurant, for the waiter to ask if you need to get away early for a movie, a play, or a review. The usual dinnertime is 7 p.m., though restaurants begin to fill up at 6 p.m.

Hollywood drives much of the southern restaurant business. Unlike the north, where a good restaurant can be a lifetime's work for a table server, this is not so common in the south. You'll see very few waiters over the age of 30. They are almost all aspiring actors. Just ask them. Ask if they are available for a screen test. Their eyes will light up with the hope that you are a talent scout. Of course they are all terribly good-looking. LA is the world's capital of good-looking people. Some of them are actually good waiters, too. Given that the restaurant trade here is so much a function of celebrity, it can be no surprise that the most successful restaurateur of the region is himself a celebrity. Nay, he is more. Wolfgang Puck is an industry. Which makes him more of a celebrity. Which enables him to be the greater industry. And so on.

Many of SoCal's crops are largely the same as NorCal's (Northern California's), though there are more citrus trees down south. Dates are grown in abundance while none come from the north. The fig is big. Tomatoes are huge, especially the vine-ripened sort. Wine grapes are grown, but not

SoCal Joke

At a Los Angeles party two people are introduced. "What do you do?" asks one. "Oh, I'm an actor," says the other. "Really?" responds the first. "At what restaurant?"

nearly so many as in the north. Salad is an industry that could support a midsized nation. As in the north, Californian-style restaurants rely on locally grown produce taken in season. But because of the longer growing season, SoCal can offer many fruits and vegetables more often throughout the year. And SoCal has a somewhat greater ethnic diversity than the north. LA is sometimes called the capital of the Pacific Rim, which is no idle boast. Nearly the whole of Latin America and East Asia are represented here. And of course, there is that lovely southland seafood (see Spiny Lobster, p159).

Classics of the South
Santa Maria Barbecue

The Santa Maria–style barbecue is perhaps the best-known and most revered of California's barbecues. It relies on strictly local ingredients, including the fuel, and so cannot be had outside San Luis Obispo county unless you truck all the stuff from there. It begins with a cut of beef known as a tri-tip. In traditional European-style butchery this is a scrap cut, left over from the carving of the loin. But the Santa Marians long ago learned how to extract the last measure of beefy goodness from this humble hunk of meat. It is rubbed with salt, pepper, and garlic, then cooked over a fire of Southern Californian red oak, and served with a salsa fresca (a fresh, chunky, tomato-based vegetable condiment) and locally grown pinquito beans (somewhat akin to kidney beans).

Driving through the county on a weekend or holiday you will smell it in every town. It is the standard celebratory feast for birthdays, graduations, victories at the ball game, finalizations of divorce, receiving the first alimony check, or being released from prison. It is a favorite fund-raising avenue for charitable or other worthy causes. Drive by a parking lot and you might see the local high school, church, Boy Scout troop, or historical society selling Santa Maria barbecued food for operating funds. Call the Santa Maria Chamber of Commerce on ☎ 805-925-2403 to see what's cooking and where during your visit.

> Sauce n. The one infallible sign of civilization and enlightenment. A people with no sauces has one thousand vices; a people with one sauce has only nine hundred and ninety-nine. For every sauce invented and accepted a vice is renounced and forgiven.
>
> *Ambrose Bierce,* The Devil's Dictionary, *1911*

Burrito

Everybody in California eats burritos. Everybody. It seems to be a statutory requirement of citizenship. But in Southern California they worship the Holy Burrito. The word burrito is the diminutive (meaning "little") for burro, the Spanish for donkey, or ass. So come to Southern California and eat a little ass. It is rather like a taco, but its tortilla is made of white-wheat flour, and is always very large and soft. Rather than being merely folded over, it is rolled and tucked at the ends to make a compact, sealed structure that can be carried to work or to school without losing the goodness within. Its original filling was simply beans, Mexican style (boiled, then fried in lard or oil, and partially mashed in the process), and generally beans are still included regardless of whatever else may go into it. Chopped

WRAPS RANT

Let me define my terms from the start. A wrap is a fashion accessory, a shawl, a sweater, a jacket, preferably made of silk velvet. Ideally, it is draped (by one's paramour, of course) around the shoulders of a woman in an evening dress who has felt a sudden chill in the night air. A wrap is a romantic thing, made to warm human flesh and bone and heart. Add an adjective – fish, let's say – and it's another thing entirely. Anyone for fish and chips?

All this is to say that neither those round flat circles of *masa* (cooked corn made into a dough or batter), nor the ones made with wheat flour, are wraps. They are tortillas. They have a long tradition in Mexico and nothing that has been added to them in recent years – not the spinach that turns them green, nor the bell peppers that tint them red – has been an improvement.

Yes, this humble staple is in trouble, and not just because the Mexican government has lifted price controls. In contemporary California the simple perfection of a tortilla has been eclipsed by the modern conceit known as a wrap, which refers both to the wrapper and to the mishmash of ingredients inside. Shiitake mushrooms, refried beans, brown rice, sun-dried tomatoes, couscous, tofu, arugula, grilled radicchio, basil oil, wasabi chutney, mango-ginger-soy salsa, all stuffed into an innocent tortilla: a wrap is convenience food at its most confused.

It's a shame. A burrito, a warm tortilla filled as it was meant to be, as they have been for centuries, with a little chopped meat, a few shrimp or some grilled fish, minced onions, a squeeze of lime, a whisper of salsa, a bit of cilantro, is a thing of absolute perfection. If you can eat it outside, near the ocean, at a vendor's cart under the Mexican full moon, all the better. If the tropical wind picks up, if the breeze turns chilly, then, and only then, will you need a wrap.

Michele Anna Jordan lives, writes, and eats in her native California

A burrito as it was meant to be

meat is a common addition, as well as tomato, salsa, cheese, sour cream, avocado, and onion. Vegetarian versions usually include rice. There was once an Englishman who ate a burrito and did not despise it.

The Mexican burrito has its child in California, and now it has its grandchild. It is called a wrap. During the 1990s Californians began filling burritos with things that are not even known in the Mexican motherland. They started wrapping Chinese stirfried dishes in a pristine white tortilla; Italian meatballs in tomato sauce might also be wrapped in a tortilla; we have seen curried lentils thus wrapped, and fried fish, and mashed taro root, and on and on.

French-Dip Sandwich

This legendary sandwich is a staple on the menus of truck stops, diners, cafeterias, and all manner of humble eateries. Elegant in its simplicity. Satisfying in its wholesome goodness. Perfect in its sensory symmetry. And a carnivore's delight. It's just meat and bread, but meat and bread in the most delicious marriage. Usually, though not always, it consists of roast beef on a semi-hard French roll, with the cut sides of the roll having been dipped in the juices of the roasting pan. Often served with french fries or coleslaw on the side, and a small pot of hot mustard, the French-dip sandwich is yet another example of Southern Californian comfort food.

To find it at its place of origin you must take yourself to Los Angeles. To 1001 North Alameda in downtown LA. There you will find the establishment that gave birth to this perennial of the California roadside board of fare. The delicatessen known as Philippe the Original opened for business in 1908 with Philippe Mathieu, a recent arrival from France, as proprietor. Then, as now, the joint was devoid of pretension, put on no airs, and intimidated no one. It did, and does, look like a sawdust saloon. Yes, that's real sawdust on the floor. Those long wooden benches and stools may actally be originals. Pickled pig's feet, chile con carne, soups, stews, puddings, and pies are now, and have always been, standards of the menu. But you must come for the taste of history.

In 1918 Officer French, an LA beat cop, came to Philippe the Original for lunch, as was his custom. He ordered a sandwich of a variety of roasted meats. As Philippe was slicing the meats and assembling the sandwich he accidentally dropped the bread roll in one of the roasting pans, soaking it with the savory juices. Hoping his customer wouldn't mind, he retrieved and used the "sullied" roll for the sandwich. The copper loved it. The next day, as the story goes, he returned with colleagues for his "French" sandwich that had been "dipped" in the roasting pan. They all acclaimed it a tasty construction, and a Californian creation had emerged.

Spiny Lobster

It's often simply called a bug. Some call him "bug ugly" but we call him a thing of beauty. *Panulirus interruptus*, or Pacific lobster, looks like a lobster who lacks claws. He has the sectional tail of a lobster, the carapace of a lobster, and actually looks like an Atlantic lobster (genus *Homarus*) that has been denuded of his crusher claws. But the Pacific Ocean dweller is actually a large crayfish. However, he is as tasty as his distant cousin and, so, worthy of the name. The spiny lobster comes in a range of colors from bright yellow with blue stripes to flaming red. His long antennae are graceful and functional. If you're a diver and you pick him up with your hand to take him home for dinner, he cannot attack you, being without claws. He's a pussycat. A sweet, succulent, delicious pussycat.

Spinies are a southern dish, as they are harvested down this way, from Baja California to San Luis Obispo. Possibly the most popular preparation is grilling the lobster in its shell, over charcoal. This helps impart the flavor of the shell into the meat, and keep it moist within the shell. It also makes a good salad with aioli dressing. In San Diego you might find it in an omelet at a Sunday brunch or breakfast buffet, or as a taco or burrito in a Mexican joint.

And of *Panulirus interruptus'* queer name? It refers to a set of grooves that transverse his tail shell. They don't quite make it all the way across the tail. They are "interrupted."

REGIONAL VARIATIONS

DON'T MISS

- Lunch at LA's Grand Central Market
- Revolving cocktails atop the Bonaventure Hotel
- Date milk shakes at Palm Springs/Indio
- The original French-dip sandwich
- Cal-Mex and margaritas at El Cholo Cafe

La Frontera (The Frontier)

When this long stretch of territory along the wild Pacific coast, from Finestierra in the south to Humboldt Bay in the north, was named California, it was subdued and made Spanish, then Mexican. In 1847 it was divided between Baja (Lower) and Alta (Upper) California. But this division was never complete. The Anglophones and Hispanophones occupying this zone have never been truly separate nor together. From early on the English speakers of the north have probed the south for riches and relaxation. Those Spanish speakers of the south have never stopped coming north for work and refuge. As they look at one another across an arbitrary line on the map, they know better than to see a clean and easy division. For there is none.

DON'T MISS

- "Aztec" cuisine in Alta Californian style
- Fish tacos on the side of the road
- Abalone steak
- Learning how to order in "Spanglish"
- A visit to the oldest winery in the Californias

Left: Local patron, Southern California

THROUGH THE GLASS BLURRY

Call it La Frontera (The Frontier), as local Mexicans do, or simply La Linea (The Line). The border between the United States and Mexico, as it exists in the Southern Californian area south of San Diego, is a cultural figment. Since September 11, 2001, beefed-up security has slowed the flow of Cuban cigars and Swiss Army Knives into the United States. However, it has done little to slow the flow of culture or cuisine – these elusive entities drift back and forth (as they have for generations) as freely as birdsong, and have created an utterly unique bicultural area that spans a coast, two countries, and two major metropolises. Envision a loose, 100-mile stretch, north to south, from San Diego's historic old town near the heart of downtown, to Ensenada, a charming seaport city on the Baja peninsula some 70 miles south of the border, and the furthest most Californians venture on a day trip to Mexico.

Across this span of borderland, despite La Linea, there is a continual interchange of people and commerce, unlike any other in the world. Nowhere else on the planet do twin million-plus-population foreign cities exist side by side. It takes less than thirty minutes to drive from the center of San Diego to the center of Tijuana, Mexico, immediately south of the border. Physically, were it not for La Linea, the two cities would have merged decades ago. Culturally, they did generations back.

At this single funnel point, some 60 million crossings are made through the international "barrier" each year for work and play, and to dine, shop, bank, and visit relatives. It is the world's busiest and, perhaps, the world's most taken-for-granted border crossing. To put that in perspective, those who nonchalantly move back and

Huevos Rancheros, Tijuana, Mexico

Mexican vineyard worker

forth between Mexico and California at this crossing equal approximately one-fifth the population of the United States. Every day the old and young walk, ride bicycles, take buses, and drive cars, north and south. With them, in both directions, goes everything Latin, everything American. Everything good, and everything bad. Money, music, food, art, language, and customs cross that border, both ways.

I can go to a restaurant in south San Diego County, or visit my bank, and hear nothing but Spanish spoken at any time of day. Early on a Saturday night, I can dine at elegant El Rey Sol in Ensenada and hear nothing but English spoken. The Mexican couples will dine later and pay in pesos. Americans pay in dollars, and the waiter doesn't even blink when making change in either currency. Or when offered a combination of both. On the northern side of the border the fast-food restaurants post their prices in both dollars and pesos.

Highway signs along the spectacular Mexican coastal drive south of Tijuana designate destinations in kilometers rather than miles, but then caution in English, "Do not throw trash." Sailors from San Diego's huge naval base heading south for a spree, and suburban day-trippers hunting down serious bargains in hand-carved furniture pause south of the border for a beer. And everybody calls it *cerveza*.

Street signs throughout Southern California read Villa de la This and El Camino de la That. Menus offer moles (moh-layz; traditional Mexican sauces), *chiles rellenos* (chee-lehs reh-yeh-nohs; stuffed peppers), and Puerto Nuevo–style lobster, and nobody needs subtitles or a translation. Mexican food is as much a part of the border culture as skateboards and tan lines, and as familiar and homelike as mariachi music.

It is a gift to both countries, this bicultural, cross-cultural haven, this easy familiarity with what would elsewhere be exotic. Everybody speaks "Spanglish," at least. Everybody eats tacos as well as hamburgers; pops jalapeno peppers; and knows the difference between a corn tortilla and a flour tortilla, and which goes with what. Everybody likes a steak with baked potato. Everybody eats french fries. And, of course, everybody here knows that *sopa* isn't soap. It's soup.

Paula McDonald lives and writes in La Frontera

The Road

It is no accident that songwriter Bobby Troup encouraged us to go on a "California trip" and to "Get your kicks on Route 66." Nowhere in America does the road have greater mystique, greater meaning, more hope, more hardship, or more that's good to eat and drink than in California. We may use superlatives aplenty to describe those wonderful things we find and direct you to. But no one can contradict us when we tell you that a two-lane road, a six-lane freeway, or an old country lane carries with it, along with all those automobiles, the hopes, dreams, and appetites of Californians of all stripes. Come to California. Get a car, or a motorcycle, and hit the road.

DON'T MISS

- Getting your kicks on Route 66
- Car-engine cookery
- Dinner in a roadhouse
- Dining in an automobile showroom
- Biscuits and gravy

The Roadhouse

This institution is as old as the automobile itself. As soon as Californians could take the wheel they were off on their Sunday drives looking for places to eat. There are no rules as to what constitutes a roadhouse, but there are shared characteristics. They are generally located outside city limits, at least when built and first opened (many have been subsequently enveloped by urban sprawl). They have a rustic feel to them, calling to mind a farmhouse, rancho, or country cottage, or even boathouse. They are always warm and welcoming, undemanding, and very giving. They are always located right on the edge of the road.

Roadhouse food is generally simple, hearty, and satisfying. Think of the best of home cooking, and send it down the road. It's heavy on meat and potatoes, and it's common to see a few Italian dishes. Fowl usually consists of roasted or fried chicken, while fish might include sautéed trout or broiled salmon. Watch for the soup of the day, a traditional salad, or a salad bar.

Wherever you are in California you are somewhere near a roadhouse. And if you are in the San Francisco Bay Area you may find one of the finest, oldest, most beloved roadhouses in the state. It is the quintessential roadhouse: Casa Orinda. It is about 20 miles east of San Francisco in the town of Orinda, which was originally a cattle-ranching community. Casa Orinda opened in 1932 at what was then known simply as Orinda Crossroads. And that's all it was, a place where two roads intersected in the midst of much meadowland. Though it opened in the depths of the Great Depression, it was an immediate success. It offered what people needed: comfort, restoration, and a good meal at a good price. It became the social focal point of the nearby ranching families, as well as a weekend destination for people from as far as San Francisco and Marin.

Roadhouses can be masculine or feminine, depending on their founders and their locations. The Casa, being founded by a Montana cowboy named Jack Snow, and situated in the middle of cattle country … well, don't look for lace curtains. However, about 10 years ago they started putting up huge floral bouquets, near the display of antique dueling pistols and buffalo guns. The place is all polished wood, with a huge fireplace dominating the center point of three rooms and a bar. The tabletops have all been branded with the official brands of local cattle ranches. Old black-and-white photos of the community as it grew over the years are on display in the entry. These are the kinds of touches you should look for in the Californian roadhouse, the kinds that reflect the local traditions, people, and economy. Look as well for longevity. At the Casa, for example, the average tenure for personnel is about 20 years. Their happiness in their workplace is reflected in their performance and the overall atmosphere of conviviality, and therefore in your enjoyment of your dinner.

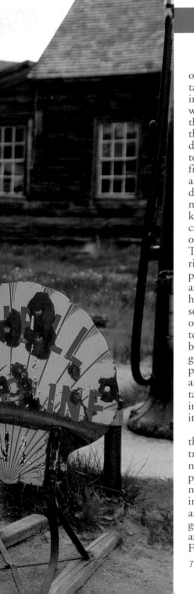

Not all roadhouses are grand, famous, or easy to find. Some are very humble and tatty. They might want paint, new plumbing, or even a new roof. But they don't want for custom, and their customers love them. There is a class of humble roadhouse that specializes in a very humble dish. A dish whose devotees will go to any lengths to try. They report to each other on their finds, giving detailed descriptions of balance, texture, and taste. It's a very simple dish – uncomplicated, but unforgiving of mistakes. It is biscuits and gravy, otherwise known as the "B&G." These are brown-crusted, fluffy, white-pan biscuits, split open to expose their moist, virgin interior. These are then smothered in a smooth, rich, creamy gravy, stoked with aromatic pork sausage and plenteous black pepper, and sometimes tarted up with wedges of hard-boiled egg. B&G is traditionally served on brown ceramic trenchers (large, oval-shaped plates, sometimes called platters), with floods of black coffee and a bottle of Tabasco sauce. And it's twice as good if you're taking it at the pitted and pockmarked laminated counter, sitting on an ancient barstool crisscrossed with duct tape to keep the springs from poking you in the butt. When B&G is properly done, it is worth a road trip.

You can find this kind of roadhouse in the most surprising places. But you might try the Flabob Airport Cafe in Roubidoux, near Riverside. Just go out to the old airport. You can't miss it. Further north, near Modesto and just off Highway 5 (I-5) in Newman, Mike's Time Out Restaurant and Lounge does a creditable job – it's good for a stop on your way between LA and Sacramento, or traveling from San Francisco to Yosemite Park.

Thinking about taking a road trip?

Manifold Destiny

In the early 19th century the Americans claimed that it was their "manifest destiny" to conquer the continent and rule from Atlantic to Pacific. "Go west, young man, go west," was the credo. And that long, long road trip from the Ohio and Mississippi Valleys to the glittering shores of California was filled with adventures, hairbreadth 'scapes, dangers and annoyances, and rich discoveries – but not much that was good to eat. We know from their journals that the marching rations of these early road-trippers consisted largely of bad bacon and camp biscuits cooked over fires of dried buffalo dung. For a treat they had prunes, which served double-duty as breakers of the gastric roadblock formed by a diet of what amounted to bacon sandwiches.

But no more! Modern Californian road-trippers have their estimable roadhouses, seaside seafood joints, sierra hideaways, and picnic fare par excellence. They also avail themselves of what is arguably the ultimate road food, the most perfect marriage of food and Ford, alimentary and automobile: cooking beneath the bonnet (under the hood). When your engine is up to operating temperature it is easily hot enough to sear your finger (should you touch it). So it is hot enough to cook a veal chop. This is not to say that you should butter your engine block and fry up steak and eggs. Rather, it is a fine means of cooking en papillote (where food is cooked in greased paper).

All packed up and ready to go

The concept is nothing new. For decades soldiers and truck drivers have punctured cans of beans and tucked them in between the exhaust manifolds of their vehicles for a hot meal on a cold day. But Californians do not take to the road for cans of beans. You can bet that on any trip down Highway 5 (I-5) you'll pass a car with a steak or a chop wrapped in layers of aluminum foil, sizzling on the six-cylinder. In the trunk (boot) is a bottle of zinfandel wine, a thick-crusted bread, and some artisanal cheese and fresh fruit. The passengers will dine in about 35 miles.

This is a perfectly safe and secure method of cookery, so long as you use common sense when it comes to dealing with hot food and hot engines. If the food is wrapped securely it will not acquire any engine crud or odors, nor will it leak and baste your block with olive oil and wine. Though if it did, it should leave a pleasant aroma along the road. It's a fine feeling to know that even as you sit placidly behind the wheel, you are doing something constructive.

There are some practical considerations for the car kitchen cook. Be sure you wrap your lunch in three layers of foil, and crimp the edges tightly. Tuck it securely into a nook or a cranny within or near the exhaust manifold. If necessary you can use a twisted length of foil to tie it down. Be sure not to block airflow or to interfere with wires. When retrieving the package be sure the engine is turned off. Neither your meal nor your extremities should come into contact with moving parts. Keep your recipes simple, and keep them relatively dry. Any recipe that calls for braising will be good for driving. Cuts of meat should be on the thin side and boneless. Use enough butter or oil to keep food from sticking to the foil.

Looking suave on the road

Whenever you go on a Californian road trip, pack a roll of aluminum foil. You will then be prepared to take advantage of any opportunity at the farmers' market, fishing docks, or local organic butcher. How smug you'll feel as you tool past the fast-food outlets, pitying the poor sods within. How satisfying when you pull into a highway rest, pop the hood (bonnet), pop a cork, and tuck in. Start your engines – on your marks, get set, cook!

Salmon Steaks with Pepper, Meyer Lemon & Haricots Verts

Those pencil-thin green beans you see everywhere in California are known as haricots verts. If you are in Los Angeles you can get them, the salmon, and the lemon at the Farmers' Market.

Ingredients

2	salmon steaks of about 6 oz (185g) each
	cracked black pepper
1	fistful of haricots verts
1	Meyer lemon
	salt
	olive oil

Sprinkle the salmon steaks liberally with cracked pepper, pressing it into the flesh on each side. Cut the lemon into 8 slices. Set 4 slices onto a well-oiled sheet of foil, and lay the steaks atop them. Lay the other 4 slices on top of the steaks. Surround the steaks with the beans, sprinkle the lot with salt, and drizzle with a little oil. Wrap tightly in three layers of foil and carefully tuck it into the engine (the engine can be either hot or cold at this time). At 60mph on Highway 5 (I-5), drive the 25 miles south from LA to Buena Vista (taking about 25 minutes). Pull over, cut the engine, and turn the salmon package over for even cooking. Drive the next 25 miles, at 60mph, to Mission San Juan Capistrano (another 25 minutes). Park under a pleasant willow tree and if you're there in March watch for the swallows to return. Lunch is served.

Serves 2

Californian Car Café

Are you in any doubt that California is the home of car culture? Or that Californians often live for the road? Sure, people eat in their cars, you say. They use their cars to find places to eat. They even cook in their cars. Here were born the drive-in movie and the drive-in restaurant. But perhaps you're still not convinced. So get in your car and drive to Oakland, the city of Jack London, Black Panthers, and Jerry Brown. Here you'll find a restaurant that you could, literally, drive into, for this restaurant sits smack dab in the middle of an automobile showroom. It's in a street called Auto Row, so-called for its mass of auto dealerships.

Carrara's Cafe is a Mediterranean-style brassiere, featuring Spanish- and Italian-inspired dishes surrounded by shiny new Jeeps and Toyotas and sexy black convertibles. The building is historic, and beautiful inside and out, with masonry and wood trim. The wine list is well thought out, the service is Johnnie-on-the-spot, and sometimes there is live music. But mostly it's the cars, beautiful new cars, begging you to take them for a spin as you dine. With every bite you are reminded that the open road is yours. Every sip of wine, every bite of chanterelle mushroom is spiced with the siren song of the open road. Perhaps, if some night when the tables are full, chef Carrara might set a service for you on the hood of a Land Cruiser. And instead of dessert, he gives you the keys. Hey, the road is all about dreams. Check it out (2735 Broadway (Auto Row) at 27th, Oakland, ☎ 510-663-2905).

shopping
& markets

When it comes to shopping in California, you can find the leading edge, the traditional, the common, and the uncommon. This is the birthplace of the supermarket, and a conservator of the farmers' market. You can even go on a guided shopping tour, sampling the tastes and aromas of gourmet neighborhoods. And of course there is always the mall.

In the home of the shopping mall it should be no surprise that shopping is a way of life. In the south it is almost a Zen experience. LA at times seems to be one big mall. Rodeo Drive in Beverly Hills is possibly the most famous shopping strip in the world. But you won't be going there for eats and drinks. It's always good to go to the source. So when in Northern California (NorCal), take yourself to the Cowgirl Creamery in Marin County (see p69). In Southern California (SoCal), check out the San Antonio Winery, the only operating winery in all of La La Land. And in La Frontera visit Bodegas Santo Tomas in Ensenada. It's the second oldest winery in the New World, and the oldest in California. In either winery, buy some drinkable history.

If you're new to California and don't know your shopping way around, one of the best ways to plunge in is to take a walking tour. In many cities tours are conducted by the local historical societies or individuals who simply have a lust for shopping and for their own special neighborhoods. The local Convention and Visitor's Bureau (CVB) will usually be able to direct you.

In San Francisco perhaps the best-known walking guide is Shirley Fong-Torres. It may be foggy outside, but the sun shines inside when Shirley enters the room. She is part cheerleader, part stand-up comic, and all teacher to those whom she guides through the boulevards, lanes, and alleyways of San Francisco's Chinatown. She can tell you history and tell you lore, but best of all she will follow her nose and lead you on a gastronomic and shopping tour of North America's second-largest Chinese community (only New York's is larger).

Fong-Torres is not the only guide here, as she has a staff of 12 guides who have led more than 100,000 people to culinary enlightenment. Even if you know nothing of Chinese gastronomy, a morning spent with one of these people will have you speaking intelligently of jasmine tea and where best to buy it, what to look for in a wok, what all those dangerous-looking Chinese kitchen implements are, the Chinese way with fish, and just how fortune cookies are made.

They don't try to promote the "exotic" per se, rather the essence of the community and its role not only as part of the city, but of the greater American family of immigrant peoples. The tour is up close and personal: participants get an opportunity to shake the hands of greengrocers, tea merchants, traditional medicine practitioners and herbalists, and restaurateurs.

Your tour through Chinatown will depend on the guide, the weather, and the season, but you might start at the green, tile-topped "Dragon's Gate" at Grant and Bush Streets. You'll proceed north on Grant, and maybe stop in at the Eastern Bakery for a piece of Chinese pastry. Thus fortified, perhaps you'll turn onto Washington Street and pass the Great China Herb Company, a good place to shop for traditional Chinese medicines and love

The Dragon Gate, entry to Chinatown, San Francisco

potions. Listen for the rattle of mahjong tiles as you pass by Spofford Alley. In nearby Ross Alley your guide may stop at the Golden Gate Fortune Cookie factory, which has been turning out these tasty little nubbins for over three decades. You are welcome to stand at the door and watch the operation at no cost. Of course you can buy their products for a few pennies each, and they will even customize your fortunes contained therein. Or you might like to try their signature specialty: "French adult fortune cookies." Sooner or later you'll end up on Stockton Street. This might well be the greatest show in Chinatown, for it is here that the locals come to shop. Live fish markets, bird markets, and grocery and fruit markets are all alive and bursting with eager shoppers and shouting vendors. This joyful chaos could be your best memory of your walk through Chinatown. Now time for lunch.

Shirley's operation, known as Wok Wiz Walking Tours and Cooking Center, offers shopping and dining tours, and cooking classes.

Wok Wiz is located at 654 Commercial Street, San Francisco, CA 94111, ☎ 415-981-8989, fax 415-981-2928, **W** www.wokwiz.com.

Farmers' Markets

Farmers' markets are some of the best places in California to see what the locals are like; what they eat and how; and what their needs and values are. In recent years they have also become one of the main means of survival for the small, family farmer, an endangered species in the USA. The most famous farmers' market in the state is doubtless that of Los Angeles, and residents take justifiable pride in it. Los Angeles' Farmers' Market is big, boisterous, and overflowing with fruits, vegetables, meat, fish, and fowl. It's also a great place for lunch or breakfast, with many small eateries. It's very popular with the local cops, so we suppose it's also a safe place to dine. This market is a permanent fixture, open all day, every day. It has a roof, but is open to the air. Across town is the Grand Central Market, which, unlike the Farmers' Market, is an enclosed venue, so is comfortable in all types of weather. And this is more of a place to eat than to shop. Farm goods are sold, but most of the commerce is in food. While there are a few Thai and Chinese stalls, most of the cooking is Mexican.

Up north, the Berkeley Farmers' Market is a weekly affair, every Saturday. This being Berkeley, you can count on a few people handing out political tracts, and buskers singing folk songs or playing bluegrass music. And Chez Panisse chefs shop here. (We're not kidding.)

Nuts for sale at the Heart of the City Farmers' Market, San Francisco

Wheatgrass at the Marin County Farmers' Market

San Francisco's Ferry Plaza Farmers' Market convenes weekly at its new premises in the restored Ferry Building, with its distinctive clock tower at the foot of Market Street. The building is graced with arched arcades that provide sidewalk and interior kiosks for growers of Northern California's seasonal and sustainably grown fruit, vegetables, and flowers. Inside the three-story, sunlit structure, a variety of shops offer some of California's best meat, poultry, fish, wine, artisan cheeses, and chocolate, as well as plenty of other goodies. The Ferry Building marketplace is also host to two casual cafés and two swanky restaurants.

SHOPPING & MARKETS

No shortage of strawberries at the Marin County Farmers' Market

BERKELEY FARMERS' MARKET

I've worked at my share of farmers' markets over the years, and as a cooking instructor and self-professed produce geek, I've shopped at even more. Therefore, I feel justified in my proclamation that the Berkeley Farmers' Market is one of the best, if not the most neuroses-laden, markets in the nation.

I started working at the market three years ago, after I fell in love with the cute puppy belonging to Frog Hollow Farm. I would stop by their stand every market to get my fix of puppy love, and thus became acquainted with Becky Smith of Frog Hollow, a talented pastry chef in her own right. Becky's partner, "Farmer" Al Courchesne, is known for growing some of the finest organic peaches and other stone fruit around. A peach, says Farmer Al, is "like sex in a fuzzy skin."

When Becky offered me a job (possibly because she took pity on my obvious doglessness), I was only too eager to accept. And so began my brilliant career as a part-time peach pusher.

If, as my personal experience can attest, waiting tables is a challenge in Berkeley, then just try selling food products at its farmers' market. At least at a restaurant people can look at the menu beforehand and have some idea of what they'll be eating (or, if you're from Berkeley, *not* eating, due to any number of food sensitivities, aversions, allergies, purported allergies, or political statements). When Becky started making organic jam and pastries from the farm's fruit, she was fulfilling a longtime dream of turning the raw ingredients growing right outside her kitchen door into edible offerings that would reflect the soul of the farm. What could be more gratifying to Frog Hollow's loyal customers, she reasoned, than handmade tarts brimming with fruit fresh from the orchard?

Well, lots of things, apparently. While we have our share of devotees who think Becky's farmstead products are perfect as they are, it seems just as many detractors will be satisfied with nothing less than fat-free, sugar-free, dairy-free anti-pastries. How many times must we hear, "Are these vegan?", "Why don't you use stevia (an herbal sugar substitute)?"

California peaches

Actually, organic sugar and sugar substitutes such as honey and stevia are often difficult to bake or make jam with because they have a different chemical composition from refined sugar.

"I can't *believe* you're suggesting serving your Asian pear chutney with *flesh*!" (hey, it tastes great with roast pork, so sue us!), "I'm diabetic – why don't you make sugar-free jam?", "How much fat is in each of these?" (it's a three-inch tart – probably not enough to send you to an early grave), and so on, ad nauseam.

When did we become such a culture of food phobics? Isn't it enough to offer a pure product, made of tree-ripened fruit, free of pesticides, hydrogenated oil, and trans-fatty acids? Why can't we just enjoy the simple, primal, sensual act of eating? Can't we all just get along?

Neurotic food nazis aside, the market is not without its share of other characters. Nearly every week, Lowell, a self-proclaimed poet, will cruise through the crowd of shoppers, wearing an eight-quart soup pot on his head, singing, "Poems, poems, who wants to hear a poem?"

There's the ever-present troupe of wanna-be Bob Dylan's, who busk at the market for spare change, belting out ballads with a sincerity that belies their obvious tone deafness. Freeloaders and freaks, homeless and housewives, children and chefs.

In spite of the occasional verbal assault from angry vegans and cranky customers, the market is a truly special place to work. To be surrounded by people so connected to the land and so committed to preserving California's precious resources, growers of produce so exquisite it ends up on the tables of some of the country's finest restaurants, and artisans of bread and cheese of a quality equal to any found in Europe; these are the reasons I stay.

For a city of over 100,000, Berkeley is an amazingly close-knit community, and the market reflects this. We know many of our customers personally, and there is a camaraderie that exists among all of the market vendors. We're a family. We support each other. I'll trade you some first-of-the-season Burlat cherries for some of your haricots verts (green string beans).

The market offers a respite from the urban racket of the city – it is an oasis of green, earthly things, a refuge from the ever-growing parade of strip malls and tract homes that threaten to take over our agricultural land. I can think of no other community so deeply dedicated to supporting sustainable agriculture, and of so many chefs and consumers enamored of cooking and eating the fresh, the seasonal, the local.

And that, in a nutshell, is why I choose to make my home in Berkeley, California. Long may she reign.

Laurel Miller, The Sustainable Kitchen
(**w** www.sustainablekitchen.com)

SHOPPING & MARKETS

Things to Take Home

If your customs agents will let you, bring home some local olive oil. It can be hard to find, as production is still small, but check specialty shops and farmers' markets. The stuff is unique, and the best here will match the best anywhere else. Wine should go without saying, and you should have no trouble with customs. Californian brandy is consumed mainly locally, so you may like to take a bottle with you. A Californian cookbook is a must. Many restaurants sell them, often signed by the author. Or if you are in town during a book festival, there will be opportunity there. Check with the local CVB.

Golden spirits of the Golden State

HOW MY BUTCHER CHANGED MY PALATE

It wasn't because Alice Waters said so. Nor was it the glossy cookbooks by the likes of Wolfgang Puck and other celebrity chefs. No, the refining of my palate from the old college days of macaroni and cheese, and hot dogs and more cheese, was because of something located right around the corner: my neighborhood butcher, Little City Meats.

Ron, my butcher, is a popular man. So too is his son Mike. Downtown executives leave their offices in a hurry, careful not to miss Ron's 5:30 p.m. closing time. Orders are called through in advance. Cars can be seen double-parking on the busy street where Little Italy sides with San Francisco's bustling Chinatown. Some of the city's finest restaurants are said to send anonymous drivers to pay homage to Ron's temple of fine meats. Sometimes they even buy in bulk. Runs are made on the extra-thick fancy bacon. Arrive too late in the week and you might be left slumping home, uttering some unacceptable reason as to why you couldn't bring home the bacon.

Ron has an assortment of sausages all made on the premises, as well as pork loin roasts; sirloin, porterhouse, rib-eye, and New York steaks; hamburgers; Italian meatballs; stuffed chicken breasts; skinny Coney Island hotdogs; and thick old-fashioned beef frankfurters. Come

Flavors of the world in California

Because California is made up of people from all over the world, you can find shops carrying goods from all over the world. Visit the local Chinatown, Japantown or Koreatown, the Little Saigon or Little Italy, or the local Latin quarter, and shop for their goods. And then there are purveyors of fine and pricey kitchen goods that anyone might like if the budget allows. One of the biggest chains of such stores is Williams-Sonoma. A cottage industry in this state is artisan potteryware. Along Highway 1, and through the northern wine country, you'll see potters' sheds. Some of the work is worthless junk, but most of it is quite good. Curiously, the junk is often the higher-priced stuff.

Thanksgiving and Christmas, he keeps a demi-glaze on hand. For Easter, he prepares a traditional lamb sausage. Whatever time it is, Ron is ready for those who feast on fine meats.

And if around the corner is too far, I'll give my butcher a call in case I failed to ask not just the cooking time but the ideal temperature. Ron encourages just a little olive oil, and quick pan-searing of the meat to complement its natural flavor.

Cuisine is about place and proximity in particular. Yet one of the ironies of modern food production is the loss of a sense of place and an understanding of where food comes from. Who needs farms when you've got supermarkets? Trucks, trains, and planes bring food from afar as well as that which is out of season. Few care how it got here, only that it is here. The shelf is seemingly its point of origin.

But a steak in a store wrapped in Styrofoam and plastic says nothing. The pleasure of a neighborhood butcher is having someone able to tell you about what you eat, where it came from, and how it should best be prepared. Some say a good butcher may be a thing of the past. I say it should also be a part of the future.

Garrett Culhane was lead photographer for World Food Vietnam

Flavored oils and vinegars, mainstays of the Californian kitchen

You should also visit a supermarket while you're in California. You can learn a lot about a place at the supermarket. When former Soviet Union premier Nikita Khrushchev visited the Golden State in 1959, he desired two things: a trip to Disneyland, and a trip to a supermarket. California invented the supermarket, and most at the time thought it a good idea.

where to
eat & drink

What's your pleasure? In California you'll find great slabs of red meat, floods of red wine, unequaled vegetarian fare, mighty fine seafood, and the leading edge of culinary thinking and creation. And for your drinking pleasure, ensconce yourself in a gilded cocktail lounge where Hollywood stars imbibe; swagger into a western saloon; chug suds in a microbrewery; or just sip a nice glass of wine.

Where to Eat
California Cuisine Restaurant

There is no such thing as a typical California Cuisine restaurant. When it comes to a proper sit-down restaurant serving what can be said to be "California Cuisine," there is simply no pigeonholing it. Each restaurant is a reflection of the personality of its driving force, be it chef, owner, designer, or all of the above. In establishments of long standing, even the waiters come to influence the character of the place. Many such places are wood-paneled and ski-lodge cozy. Some look like a Tuscan villa or a Mexican patio. They can be grand and glorious with fluted columns and Art Deco chandeliers; bare, spare industrial chic; hushed or full of hubbub; Mission revival; urban survival; Chez Panisse rival. So let's have a look at Chez Panisse, where, it is said, it all started.

It's a converted house, in a rather average neighborhood in the university town of Berkeley, and within walking distance of the University of California campus. There are several other fine eateries nearby, and they all make up what locals call the "Gourmet Ghetto." On Chez Panisse's ground floor is the main dining room, with the set menu changing daily and ranging in price from about $40 to $75; reservations are necessary. Upstairs is the more casual Chez Panisse Café with an à la carte menu that changes with availability; reservations are not taken.

Immediately you enter Chez Panisse you will notice something most California Cuisine restaurants share: a feeling of casual, undemanding elegance. Décor is carefully thought out, doesn't scream for your attention, doesn't compete with the food or your companions, yet still is comfortably in evidence. In the case of Chez Panisse it's all rich but simple wood, and ample floral arrangements. Several wooden tables occupy the center of the room, and wooden banquettes (with cushions for soft seating) surround all. Waitstaff are neat and well groomed, plainly dressed. No one wears a tie at Chez Panisse. In fact, you can dine in a clean, pressed T-shirt and a pair of jeans. But that's Berkeley. Don't try it across the bay in San Francisco.

Dinner will reflect what is available locally and within season. It is not unheard of for the tomatoes in your salad, for example, to have arrived that morning quite unexpectedly from a backyard grower. The story could easily go as follows:

Foraging in the herb garden of the Culinary Institute of America

Preparing for the first sitting at Chez Panisse

FELONS & FODDER

Arugula grown by ex-cons, and Snickers Bar Pies concocted by ex-addicts? Well, this is San Francisco, where Project Open Hand, founded by Ruth Brinker, started a trend way back in the 80s by delivering high-end food free to HIV patients.

Next under that hoary "only in San Francisco" heading comes The Garden Project, which began in 1992 as a post-release program whereby former prisoners could earn a living by growing organic vegetables for poor communities. To generate income, tarragon and fancy salad greens like arugula and frisée leaves were also sold to high-end restaurants.

Catherine Sneed and San Francisco's sheriff Mike Hennessey successfully set up and expanded the project. Although the greens-for-gourmets plan was a hit, The Garden Project no longer sells vegetables to restaurants. Instead it donates its harvests solely to good food banks and family charities.

Meanwhile, dining under the arches of Bay Bridge at Delancey Street Restaurant on the Embarcadero has long been a "feel-good"

Harvesting the tomatoes, the grower discovered that they were quite possibly the best the good earth had ever yielded and must, perforce, be offered to the temple. With his yield of a single box he showed up at the kitchen door to await the final judgment. When the high priest/chef determined that they were indeed the best the good earth had ever produced, the grower was offered a choice: money or dinner. If he was wise he took the dinner.

Your dinner will be composed bit by bit over a span of days and weeks. In constant consultation with suppliers, the chefs will have planned, replanned, and fine-tuned right up to this day. Vegetables will have been in the ground only hours ago, while ham might have been curing for 18 months. Cheese might have been made the day before, or have been aging since last season. Fish will have been flapping on the boat deck in the predawn, and your recommended wine might be older than your waiter. That waiter can tell you anything you may wish to know about any dish you are served, and you will be served with quiet professionalism. And what you are served is excellence, of the highest order. What you are served is the work of people who are more demanding of themselves than we will ever be. And you will be served in an atmosphere of mirthful reverence, reserved enthusiasm, repartee that never intrudes upon the eating and drinking, a shared experience of some of the best that life has to offer to mere mortals. And that's just one restaurant.

thing to do, thanks to Mimi Silbert, the widow of Delancey Foundation crusader John Maher. In his short but heroic life, Maher did more to rehabilitate the homeless, alcoholics, jailbirds, and drug-addicted of the city than anyone, and Mimi still runs his self-help residential homes for people trying to start again. Sadly, Maher died young; but Mimi has carried on his work. Ten years ago she launched this remarkable restaurant, which trains some of the foundation's residents in restaurant management, including cooking and serving meals. She also gave the menu here its two most popular desserts, the Snickers Bar Pie and Herbie's Pie, both also available at the foundation's Crossroads Café around the corner. Some of the city's most distinguished chefs have pitched in by helping plan the menus for Delancey trainees, who sign on for a two-year course before graduating to a new life. Delancey Street glows with fresh produce and bonhomie; it's almost always full, even on early weeknights. Sometimes the food can be uneven and the service a little slow. But the staff try so hard it doesn't matter.

Elgy Gillespie lives and writes in San Francisco

Steak House

It's undeniable that California is thought by many to be a land of lotus eaters, a population of tofu-touting organic vegetarians, vegans, and other food fetishists. And that is all true. But it is equally true that this is one of the biggest meat-eating populations in the world. And not just in the road-houses, rural byways, and cattle-ranching districts. Even the politically correct can eat food that had parents. Since the days of the rancheros, Californians have loved their beef and still do. To be sure, there was a brief time in the 1990s when the steak house went ignored by the trendy. But those trendy have trended away and the steak house is still with us. To our knowledge, the only city of any importance that lacks a steak house is Berkeley. But Berkeley we can forgive.

From north to south it is one of the most enduring kinds of restaurant in California, a culinary constant that has proven immune to financial ups and downs, political swings left or right, cultural zigs and zags.

A typical dinner in a fine steak house begins with entry into the premises. Immediately you notice that you have entered another realm, one where calm and dignity reign, which is not to say stuffiness. Autographed photos of celebrities likely hang in the reception area, and the mirthful sounds of feasting will roil out to you. But first, a visit to the bar. Here you'll find a ball game on TV with the sound turned off, padded bar stools, and a bartender wearing a vest and tie. Perhaps a display of old pistols hangs from the wall. Ceremony calls for a martini, for cold gin and hot beef are the order of the night.

Take your table, and receive with all due aplomb the leather-bound menu. It will be heavy, but blessedly short. Usually it carries up to a dozen cuts of beef, perhaps one of lamb, and a smoked pork chop. It will include some kind of shellfish (lobster is typical), a finfish such as halibut, and perhaps a pasta dish. Creamed spinach is the most traditional vegetable side dish, followed by steamed broccoli and grilled asparagus. A baked potato is almost obligatory, but mashed potato is often on offer, or french fries; and here and there fettuccini alfredo. Desserts are simple: rice pudding, apple pie, peach cobbler, homemade ice cream.

A Caesar salad or a tossed salad is the way to begin. Your waiter will wheel the salad cart to your table and prepare it before your eyes. Thus begins the dinner theater. You've finished your martinis, you're tucking into your salads, and you've no doubt ordered a bold red wine. Or, if you prefer, no one will complain if you call for beer, or even iced tea. Steaks will be brought to you on the plate. If you've ordered roast of prime rib (and at some time you should) it may come to you on a silver, torpedo-shaped cart and be carved at tableside into shimmering red slabs of rare beef. Clinking of glasses, clicking of cutlery, and moans of delight complete the scene.

A few practicalities: There are a number of national steak house chains, and we have nothing ill to say of them. We have enjoyed many a good meal in some of them. But for real character, our best advice is to find those old local favorites of long standing. In San Francisco we happily recommend Harris' and the House of Prime Rib as establishments that breathe the Gold Rush spirit of The City by the Bay. In LA nothing captures the glitz and glamor better than LA Prime, atop the Bonaventure Hotel. For a protein fix with the best view in town, you can't go wrong. And in San Diego, the granddaddy of all steak houses is Rainwater's on Kettner; everything a steak house ought to be and then some.

Portions will be huge, so consider ordering the smallest cuts. If you're still hungry you can have another side dish, or even an extra dessert. And be aware that certain establishments have been known to take advantage of male vanity. "Yes sir. Tonight we have the He-Man Special at $40, and the Ladies' Petite Cut at $23. Which can I bring you?" Learn from us, and save that $17.

You won't leave hungry after dining at a Californian steak house

Seafood House

A typical Californian seafood restaurant might be thought of as a steak house that serves fish. In New England it might be a cozy chowder house. In New York it's likely to be elegant and on the top floor of some tall building. Whereas in the Deep South the best seafood will be in a gorgeous, old, colonial-era pile in the French Quarter of New Orleans. But in California seafood is taken in an atmosphere of frontier egalitarianism, conviviality, and mirth. As old as the steak house tradition is on the Left Coast, the seafood house is even older, as old as the Gold Rush. You could drive the coast highway from San Diego to Pelican Bay and eat nothing but splendid fish in any number of seafood restaurants. Virtually anywhere that a wharf, however small, insinuates itself into the waves, there or very nearby you will find a Californian seafood restaurant.

While they do have their degrees of sophistication and cost, and locations can range from smack dab on the beach to midtown, there are some norms. Your typical Golden State seafood joint takes its décor cue from the old wharf. The warehouse look of a dockside sail locker turned cannery-row eatery is what many strive for: big, open space with lots of brightwork, nautical hodgepodge and the smell of the sea. A lot of good photographs of landing piers, fish, and fishing boats, will hang on the walls. A bustling kitchen is often separated from the dining room by large window panes, so as to provide for a colorful dinner theater.

The menu is often a foot and a half long and you probably had no idea that there were so many species of, and so many ways to prepare, fish, fish, fish. Creatures that walk upon the land or soar the skies are little in evidence, of course. But there is usually a hamburger available, as kids are sometimes chary of sea dwellers. There is always a steak, but this can be said of virtually any non-vegetarian restaurant in the state. And nowadays most places offer a vegetarian dish, usually pasta, and a range of salads or a salad bar, steamed broccoli or carrots, coleslaw, potatoes, rice, and good bread. Desserts tend to be simple: carrot cake, pies, custards, and ice cream.

But then there is the fish (and shellfish). There will be a full range of Pacific coast catch: halibut, scallops, swordfish, salmon, shrimp, and on and on and on. While the emphasis is the marine, the riparian is not ignored, and most establishments will offer brook trout, lake bass, marsh crayfish, and the like. Many will also offer Right Coast imports such as Maine lobster, and while a few may still carry Chilean sea bass, these days many are choosing to remove it from the menu (see p61). Salt cod from the Mediterranean is making appearances, and some chefs are actually curing their own, using locally caught rock cod. If you see it on the menu we encourage you to give it a go.

Whatever you select for dinner, preparations tend toward simplicity. In keeping with the steak house ethos of being "user friendly," the fish house is

Fisherman's Wharf, San Francisco

not the place to go for Napoleon-type presentations – what has come to be known in California derisively as "tall food." There are no special sauces in the fish house. You've got your ketchup, your tartar sauce, your cocktail sauce, and your creamed horseradish, maybe a malt vinegar, Tabasco sauce, and Worcestershire sauce. A few dishes will be served with a butter sauce cooked in the pan. You might get a hollandaise, but you probably wouldn't want it. The most complex preparation in this sort of place will be in the family of fish stews: French bouillabaisse, Greek *kakavya*, Californian cioppino, or the like. In the south, look for *sopa de siete mares* (seven seas soup), a Mexican-inspired version of fish stew.

While the great majority of seafood restaurants in California are of Western tradition, there are many Chinese restaurants that specialize in fish. Most of them are found in the Chinatowns of San Francisco and Los Angeles, but the Silicon Valley and the central coast areas are also blessed with good Chinese fish houses. Japanese sushi places are common too. In the 1980s they were almost a plague, but now sushi is no longer a fashion statement. It's just good food.

It's usually easy to know if you've encountered a seafood house, whether on the street or in the phone book. The name is a dead giveaway. You'll rarely find one named Chez Louis, or Joe's Fine Food. It will have a thematic name, and sometimes even a whacky one: The Chart House, The Beach House, The Captain's Cabin, Ocean Star, Star of China Seafood House, Anthony's Star of the Sea, The Reel Inn, Neptune's Net, The Fisherman's Folly. Keep a weather eye out, shipmate. There's plenty more where those come from.

Bar & Grill

It's just what the name says. At its simplest, it's a sawdust saloon that happens to have a grill near the bar. There could be a retired truck driver, or a prison trustee, or a woman of a certain age slinging hash, flipping burgers, breaking eggs, and worrying over a pot of chile con carne. An ancient jukebox will play hits by Elvis, Patsy Cline, and Sinatra. A pool table is de rigueur, especially if the felt is worn in places, and none of the cue sticks are perfectly straight. Most of the patrons drink beer from long-neck bottles. You should be able to get a margarita if you don't ask for the frozen variety, but requests for a cosmopolitan will be laughed at. Ask for a sidecar, a negroni, or a grasshopper and you'll only cause confusion. But, this being California, you can get a martini, and you can have a nice glass of wine. It might only be jug wine or it could be something better; depends on what the owner likes. Even if it is only jug wine, it's Californian jug wine and so it's pretty good for the money.

Your burger, or your chile, or your chile burger, or your bacon and eggs, will generally be served at the bar, and you might eat it there or take it to a table. And if you are in even the humblest establishment you will likely find this to be damned fine food for its type. A sawdust bar & grill relies on its regular customers for its survival. It isn't going to be visited by newspaper restaurant reviewers wearing silly disguises to protect their anonymity. It isn't going to be listed in tourist brochures or honored with membership in the local chamber of commerce. The chill of its beer, the savor of its simple food, and the homey ambiance are what keeps the regulars coming back. Thus it could be viewed as being at the bottom of the dining scale. But that's not a criticism by any means.

At the other end are fabulous houses of bar & grill degustation. Operated by alumni of Alice Waters and Wolfgang Puck, housed in historic buildings, and decorated by inspired designers, they are jewels of the community. They are houses of mirth, cultural lodestones, venues of personal repair and restoration. And they can be pretty pricey. Yet when you enter such a place, regardless of how grand, you know immediately that you are in a bar & grill. Like the steak house and the fish house, the bar & grill is without pretension. It is a welcoming, happy place. The furnishings tend to be on the heavy side. There is a definite masculine feel, but with feminine undertones. As with its poorer sibling, there is a full bar with some kind of cookery going on within sight. The full kitchen is in another space, but behind or near the bar will be a grill, a woodfired oven, or maybe a mesquite charcoal barbecue, sizzling with salmon steaks and venison chops, as well as marinated giant asparagus, sweet Maui onions or heads of brightly bitter radicchio.

The menu will be heavy on meat, but not as much as a steak house; it will include fish, but not as much as a fish house. The high-end bar & grill might be thought of as a hybrid of the two. Very often the bar & grill will offer chops and fowl that have been smoked in-house. Some of these places maintain their own gardens and so a wide range of salads will be on the menu. If a woodfired oven is operating you can count on pizza. Not the sort you would find at a pizzeria, but flights of fancy limited only by the chef's whimsy. And sweets can be very elaborate. You won't see a pool table. But you can get a long-neck beer. And that retired truck driver, or prison trustee, or woman of a certain age, just might be dining next to you.

Sand dabs and a martini at Tadich Grill – you can't get more San Francisco than that

Californian breakfast, Sarafornia Restaurant, Calistoga

Where to Drink

This is the most bibulous state in the union. So if you can't find a good place to drink, then perhaps you're actually in the state of Utah, or maybe just in another state of mind. Here is the largest wine industry in the New World, a brewing industry that came with the Gold Rush, the leading edge of an emerging tea culture, and a coffee culture that predates that of Seattle. Add to that the return of the Cocktail Nation and an addiction to spring water. This is a state of liquid lovers.

Brewpubs are the place to look for unique beer

One point to note: Driving under the influence of alcohol will get you a mighty big ticket in California. During holidays, sobriety checkpoints can spring up on the highways or in midtown. Smokey means business. Take public transport or assign a designated driver.

Get your Irish up here: The Buena Vista Café, San Francisco

WHERE TO EAT & DRINK

Cocktail Lounge

Always attempting a certain elegance, usually succeeding and sometimes comically missing the mark, cocktail lounges places tend to be rather quiet and very dark inside. So dark that you need to let your eyes adjust before trying to navigate your way to a table or the bar. In SoCal (Southern California), this is often a good thing because the sun can be bright, and the traffic so nerve-jangling that the cool, dark calm of a cocktail lounge is the perfect remedy. The bar usually runs the length of the room, and is faced by little cocktail tables and heavily padded chairs, banquettes, and booths. This kind of establishment runs the gamut for class and quality. They are in working-class neighborhoods and highly toned housing estates. You'll find them on waterfronts, mountain tops, downtown, uptown, across town, and around.

This being California, personal expression is a virtue, even in the design of cocktail lounges. There are those decorated in a single color, such as the Red Room, or the all black of Martuni's, both in San Francisco. In SoCal they often have a Mexican flair, a mariachi jukebox, and décor so gaudy it feels like you've just walked into a velvet painting. Many cocktail lounges are found on upper floors to provide a view. Don't miss the one in the Westin Bonaventure Hotel in downtown LA. It revolves on its axis once every hour. The lounge in the LA Four Seasons Hotel has a different kind of view: one that is thick with celebrities.

The revolving Bona Vista Lounge at the Westin Bonaventure Hotel, Los Angeles

Wine Bar

It is a common notion that California is possessed of numerous wine bars, places wherein patrons may enjoy a range of wines from a range of regions, by the glass or by the bottle. And, indeed, there are wine bars. There are even those that specialize in sparkling wines. They have names like the Bubble Lounge. Wine bars tend to be richly paneled, not too intimidating, and not cheap. But you are likely to find more of them in London, or even Bangkok (seriously), than in Californian cities. Upon reflection this should make perfect sense. Will you find many wine bars in Spain, France, or Italy? No, you will not. As in those countries, California is a place where wine is assumed to be available almost everywhere. Even a cheap saloon will offer you a decent glass of wine. To many Californians a wine bar would be on a par with a whiskey bar, or a vodka bar. Maybe not a bad idea, but one whose time has not yet come. But the point is, almost any watering hole is a wine bar by default. Cheers.

Faz Restaurant and Bar at the Marriott Hotel, San Diego

Hotel Bar

California's historic grand hotels provide for some of the most gorgeous, dramatic, artistic, glamorous and civilized boozing anywhere in the world. To say that they are ornate would be an understatement. They reflect the wealth, exuberance, and adventure of the Gold Rush, Hollywood, and the Cadillac Desert. Nay, they don't reflect, they flaunt! And to imbibe in these places is to imbibe the history of one of the grandest, quirkiest, most colorful and contradictory places on Earth. The Westin Saint Francis and the Palace Hotel in San Francisco, the Millennium Biltmore Hotel in Los Angeles, and the Hotel del Coronado near San Diego are all alive with California ghosts.

POTABLE, n. Suitable for drinking. Water is said to be potable; indeed, some declare it our natural beverage, although even they find it palatable only when suffering from the recurrent disorder known as thirst, for which it is a medicine. Upon nothing has so great and diligent ingenuity been brought to bear in all ages and in all countries, except the most uncivilized, as upon the invention of substitutes for water. To hold that this general aversion to that liquid has no basis in the preservative instinct of the race is to be unscientific — and without science we are as the snakes and toads.

Ambrose Bierce,
The Devil's Dictionary, *1911*

Enjoying a drink outdoors at the Bonaventure Hotel's bar

Drink in the opulence at the Biltmore Hotel's bar

A drink at the Del Coronado Hotel's bar guarantees a great ocean view

In such places, the Academy Awards were born; crooner Al Jolson died; King Edward VIII met Mrs. Simpson; Tony Curtis pursued Marilyn Monroe in the movie *Some Like It Hot*; Caruso survived the earthquake of 1906; President Reagan entertained Queen Elizabeth; and Green Goddess salad dressing was invented. Even if you're staying in a youth hostel or a pup tent, you should make it a point to sip some of California's unique history and culture in one or more of these living museums.

A CIVILIZED SIP

Even California's railroad is full of romance and good things to eat and drink. In the sconce-lit elegance of the Pacific Parlor Car aboard Amtrak's *Coast Starlight*, the wine steward reads aloud from her tasting notes as the green hills of Steinbeck country roll by. The afternoon wine tasting is in progress, and the oak bar is bedecked with Napa whites and Baja California reds. This movable feast of the grape takes place every day on the route between LA and Seattle, featuring hard-to-find vintages and lesser-known vintners from throughout the New World. "We believe in life beyond chardonnay," says the steward. Train travel was never so fine.

For more details, phone ☎ 1-800-USA-RAIL.

Brewpub

A brewpub is a pub that brews its own beer. There are brewpubs all over the English-speaking world, including California, where they are the same thing, only different. They might brew only one beer, but more likely they produce a range of suds, and will be continually experimenting with others. Older brewpubs often have the "older brewpub" look about them: sparse décor, plain furnishings, plenty of elbow room. Should they serve food it will be Californian pub grub: chile con carne, nachos, burgers, hot dogs, and, this being California, some kind of salad.

But many brewpubs are hardly recognizable as such to the immigrant eye. Don't be surprised to see focaccias, baked vegetable dishes, soups, and a woodfired oven issuing forth gourmet pizzas. Creative sandwiches are limited only by imagination. Many brewpubs have a proper sit-down restaurant operation going as well. In the south, the specialty might be barbecue, in the north, California Cuisine or even Spanish fare. A brewpub may be perched on the beach, nestled downtown or, most often, in your neighborhood. They can be downright posh, or artistic. We've seen them with lovely murals gracing the walls, elegant floral bouquets, or with beer gardens in the back dotted with sculpture. It would seem that the only constant among brewpubs is that they make their own beer that you may drink at the bar. Not a bad constant.

The ThirstyBear Brew Pub, San Francisco

Saloon

Yep, the good old-fashioned American West saloon is alive and well. Oftentimes it even has those swinging doors through which drunken cowboys were thrown out onto the dusty street at high noon. Plain wooden furniture, sawdust on the floor, perhaps a chandelier made from a wagon wheel hanging from the high ceiling, a long wooden bar with nicks and scars, and a barman with a mustachio – all these hallmarks of the frontier watering hole are still there for your drinking enjoyment. There are a few minor changes to be found in modern-day saloons, however: the piano player of old has been replaced by a jukebox, and the dance-hall girls have gone to school and become lawyers and scientists and even county sheriffs. But you can still order a shot of red-eye (whiskey), and the bartender will know what you mean. Sometimes they actually do offer a "free lunch", or a buffet of finger foods and sandwiches at the end of the day. One of the most beloved establishments of this genre is Heinold's First and Last Chance Saloon, in Oakland at Jack London Square. And this was, indeed, Mr. London's regular watering hole.

Many older saloons like to maintain a strict sense of frontier egalitarianism. And they have their ways of unstuffing a shirt or bending a nose held too high. If you are a gentleman, never wear a necktie into a saloon. There are those saloons where the bouncer or chief bartender will come up to you and unceremoniously cut it off with a pair of scissors and hang it from the rafters with all the others they've snipped. Then there are those where this act will be performed with much ceremony. Either way the house will laugh uproariously. If this happens to you, be a good sport about it. Only good sports are allowed in the saloon. If you are a person who puts on airs, it won't be for long. A common feature of the sound system in saloons is a microphone behind the bar that runs to a speaker in the restroom. Having a randy bartender whisper sweet nothings while thus occupied will take the airs out of anyone, especially when you return and hear the entire house repeating the bartender's musings. But for all this enforced humility, they will not throw you out through the swinging doors at high noon.

Theme Bar

These places often seem as though they all began as the same kit, to which nuances of décor were added and the selections on the jukebox tailored. They tend to be spacious, with a handsome bar that is often horseshoe shaped, paneled walls, brass rails, and other brightwork. They are happy places with gregarious patrons making a bit of noise. They are the aesthetic opposite of the cocktail lounge.

Sports Bar

Perhaps the most common theme bar is the sports bar. Here several TV sets (a dozen is common) will be showing various sporting events, with the sound turned up whenever the home team is playing. The place is festooned with team jerseys, caps, and sports memorabilia. It might have concocted special cocktails named for local sports heroes. During important games the patrons will cheer lustily when the home team scores, and the place will burst into pandemonium if they win. If they lose, the joint can turn sepulchral.

Taking in a game at the Grand Avenue Sports Bar, Biltmore Hotel

Cantina

The cantina is another popular theme, and of course will bear no resemblance to its Mexican forebear, traditionally a very humble establishment. Mexican calendars will hang on the walls, as well as bullfight posters, and neon beer signs rendered into Spanish. The bar will sling a lot of margaritas, Mexican beers with a wedge of lime stuffed into the neck of the bottle (an original California touch), and a wide range of tequilas. As often as not, no one on staff will speak more than a few words of Spanish.

Gay Bar

While the popular conception of a gay bar is of a dark, garishly decorated place full of homoerotic goings-on, these places are more likely to be closer to the theme bar. This is not to say that there are no dark, garishly decorated places full of homoerotic goings-on, but a typical gay bar is more likely to be almost distressingly normal. Perhaps the most famous gay bar in the state is Harvey's, in San Francisco. It's decorated with political memorabilia, neighborhood snaps, posters, and baseball caps. And it serves pub grub. Upon entering you might think you've stumbled into a sports bar.

WHERE TO EAT & DRINK

Options for eating and drinking in the wine country are plenty

Country & Western Bar

The country & western bar has only the remotest relationship to the saloon. It looks like any other theme bar but is full of people dressed like urban cowboys. Of course they are not cowboys, they are blue-collar workers, clerks, insurance adjusters, cops, grocers, and the occasional lawyer. But the herds of pick-up trucks corralled outside will tell you where their hearts are. There may indeed be a mechanical bull for you to ride. There will be music of Nashville. And there will be much back slapping and good-ole-boy behavior. If there is a dance floor there will be country line dancing, and perhaps free lessons in the art on certain nights of the week. Yeeha!

Music Bar

Don't expect to hear string quartets in the music bar. Nor will you hear accordion concerts, ukulele bands, or harmonica duets. The music here, for the most part, will be jazz, blues, or contemporary rock. Music bars are often situated in older buildings with cheaper rents. But don't look for them to offer cheap drinks, and do expect to pay a cover charge after 8 p.m. Don't ask for fancy drinks here. And don't expect service of a high polish. You might get it. And you might get a well-mixed, if uncomplicated, drink. Or you might get a glass of indifference from a bored scullion too hip to care. Hopefully the music will be good.

Pub

If you're reading this book you probably live somewhere in the English-speaking world. And if you're reading this section of the book it's a good bet that you plan to lift a few when in California. So we assume you know what a pub is. A pub is a pub is a pub. The accents and the temperature of the beer may change, but darts is darts and pies is pies and Guinness is stout the world over. 'Nuff said.

Vegetarians & Vegans

It is quite possible that California counts more vegetarians and vegans per capita than any other state in the union. So at first glance it would seem ironic that strict vegetarian restaurants are not very common. Indeed, outside the San Francisco Bay area and Greater Los Angeles they are almost unknown. They do exist, of course. But they tend to be small, storefront-type places, with perhaps five tables, an exposed cooler full of politically correct juice drinks, such as wheatgrass, and possessed of a strong odor of coffee, orange-scented tea, or curry. The menu is heavy on legumes, wholegrain bread, brown rice, yogurt, and dried fruit. The vastly tattooed young waiter is very friendly, and may even sit down to chat with patrons at the next table while you wait to give your order. The cook may seem to be in a deep meditative state while stirring a pot of lentils. Reservations are not taken, and coat and tie are not required. These places are most common along the far northern coast around Eureka, and the central coast around Santa Cruz.

A vegetarian micro greens salad

Most Golden State vegetarians, just like their carnivorous counterparts, demand a good feed and a little bit of style. And they generally don't want to feel exiled to some plant food wilderness where postprandial entertainment threatens to be chanting and drumming in a circle. No, no, a thousand times no! The upshot for the Golden State diner is that any restaurant of repute is vegetarian to one degree or another. Vegetarians may go to virtually any sit-down restaurant in California and order a satisfying meal from the regular menu. In some establishments, as much as 60% of the menu will be vegetarian. This is especially true of Chinese and Indian restaurants, both of which are plentiful. Western-style restaurants have almost obligatory vegetarian pasta dishes, a range of salads, mushrooms in season, baked squashes and eggplant (aubergine), pilafs, and pies. Dishes of steamed mixed vegetables dressed with olive oil or an emulsion sauce are

Juicey Lucy's organic juice bar in North Beach, San Francisco

popular, and people do astonishing things with tofu (bean curd). Even many Mexican restaurants will offer vegetarian dishes, a thing unheard of in Mexico.

There are, as well, some very fine, indeed world-class, vegetarian restaurants here. Greens Restaurant in San Francisco is the original gourmet vegetarian house in California. Also in San Francisco is the vegan place Millennium. In either, the most dedicated carnivore could have a satisfying meal and not be fully aware that he or she had eaten nothing with a face. Here you'll find no health food, no hippie food, just top-notch cookery without animal products. At both, the cooking style is Mediterranean-inspired Californian. The breads and wines are especially noteworthy. In LA, the Buddhist Chinese restaurant Fragrant Vegetable turns out rich and robust vegetarian fare, and specializes in tofu textured to resemble meat. Greek restaurants anywhere in the world will offer good plant foods, and California has several such restaurants, especially in the south. So if you're vegetarian, you'll be right at home eating out in California.

a californian
banquet

So you want to bring the Golden State home for dinner? You want some California dreamin' in the dining room? Then you've got to have some Californian wine and good bread. To add authenticity, serve up fruits and vegetables common to California, such as artichokes or avocados. But remember, the soul of California Cuisine is improvisation. Serve up that edible jazz.

So now you want to entertain California style. Cool, dude! We recommend that you take one of two approaches: casual alfresco, or something terribly civilized within doors. You won't have to wait long for a sunny day, so plan now for the outdoor feast. As much as Californians are wine lovers, they also love their beer and "designer waters." So have plenty on hand when the guests arrive. If you are within California's borders and are trying to show your wine savvy, pour them something terribly fine or something terribly ordinary. At this stage don't mess with Mr. In-Between. Give them the best of the best, or the best of the worst. Yes, if you won't be pouring something like a Schramsberg sparkler or a super premium varietal, then pour a jug wine (plonk). If you've read the Drinks chapter of this book, you'll know that even jug wine is damned good stuff, and your knowledge of it is indication of your savvy.

A LITTLE IGNACIO, PLEASE

The nacho is a bastard child conceived in the Mexican kitchen, adopted by Tex-Mex, and embellished and beatified by Cal-Mex. Sainthood should not be far away. At its most elemental it is nothing more than a corn chip dressed with cheese, tarted up with salsa, and perhaps adorned with fried beans. It may be further cloaked with sour cream, bejeweled with chives, enriched with meat, decked out with slices of olive, and perfumed with cilantro (coriander). It can be either the temple virgin or the painted lady of Cal-Mex cuisine. At fast-food places and convenience stores it is the neighborhood tramp. You will not find it in Mexico except where Americans and Canadians tend to loiter. Northern Mexicans do enjoy a breakfast torta, a semi-hard roll that is sliced in two and toasted, which is similar to the nacho. It is then spread with frijoles refritos (refried beans) and topped with cheese or avocado or both, and maybe a bit of salsa.

The nacho's origin is largely unknown to the general population, but the diligent researchers of the *Oxford English Dictionary*, and the archivists of the Church of the Redeemer in Eagle Pass, Texas, have been able to shed some light on the matter. It was in Texas in 1943 that a certain group of "ladies who lunch" went on a shopping trip to the Mexican town of Piedras Negras, just below the US-Mexican border. They decided to lunch at the Victory Club, where Señor Ignacio Anaya reigned over the kitchen. As with Caesar Cardini and the Caesar salad (see p35) he was short of goods at that moment. So he cooked up some corn chips, slathered them with what he had, no doubt liberally lubricated the ladies with liquor, and served them his famine fare. The ladies loved it. Either they or he, the record does not specify, named it for Ignacio. But they used the diminutive: Nacho.

CALIFORNIAN BANQUET

You cannot go wrong by starting off with nachos. The simplest form of nachos is simply to pile corn chips on a platter, then cover them with salsa and grated cheese. You can add whatever else you may like. Sliced jalapeño peppers, sour cream, sliced black olives, and shredded roasted pork are common additions. Trout fishermen just open a bag of chips, remove about a third of the volume, then pour in salsa, cheese, and whatever else, close the bag and shake the whole mess. You don't want to do this at your banquet, unless you are entertaining trout fishermen. For your banquet you should dress your nachos individually, so that they appear like canapés. Your guests will be most impressed, and won't have to clean their hands afterward. Simply spread each corn chip with a layer of frijoles refritos, then some cheese and perhaps guacamole, then whatever else you like. Offer this tasty appetizer with margaritas and you are on the road to success.

You will find nachos all over California. They are on offer in Cal-Mex restaurants, pubs, diners, microbreweries, amusement parks, and carnivals. They are often quite good at all these places. In convenience stores they are offered in self-serve mode. You get a little paper dish of corn chips. Then you are invited to dress this mess with a selection of sliced jalapeño peppers, industrial-grade salsa, tinned sliced olives, and a melted "processed cheese" product pumped from a machine that looks like it might do good service in a garage to dispense axle grease. It might even taste of axle grease. Which could be an improvement. But a good and freshly made nacho is amusement in your mouth.

Very Californian fare

Napa Valley wine auction, St. Helena

At this point Golden Staters will desire a pot of chile or a barbecue. If you've read this far you know how to do both. If you barbecue you should also include some vegetables. Simply quarter some onions and bell peppers (sweet capsicums), split some leeks or scallions (spring onions), slice a head of radicchio, brush them with oil and throw them onto the grill. You can do the same with fresh ears of corn, and serve them sprinkled with red pepper flakes. Close the meal with a bowl of fresh fruit and an artisanal cheese. If you're doing this outside California and your guests are Californians, play the music of the Beach Boys and see if they cry.

For an evening repast, welcome your guests with well-shaken martinis. Or if you don't want that well lubricated, offer them a crisp white wine. Sauvignon blanc is a common starter. A traditional Californian hors d'oeuvre is rumaki. Originally created by some Chinese chefs in Hawaii, and then given a Japanese name, it's perfect for the polyglot that is California. While there are variations from plain to fancy, at its simplest it's a water chestnut wrapped in bacon, stuck with a toothpick and broiled (grilled). Elegant in its simplicity, rumaki goes well with either gin or white wine.

Upon migrating to the table, you might start with soup, for the Californians love their soup, and use it as a measure of kitchen competence. They will tell you outright that if you can't make a decent soup they don't want you in the kitchen. So listen up, and seduce these demanding Californians with an artichoke soup. They are utterly defenseless against this alimentary onslaught. California is the nation's only commercial source of artichokes, and the locals feel very attached to them.

Artichoke Soup

Ingredients

3 tbs	olive oil
3	cloves garlic, crushed
12	baby artichokes or 6 large artichoke bottoms, quartered
1 tsp	hot red pepper flakes
	juice of 1 lemon
6 cups	beef stock

Heat olive oil in a large saucepan over medium heat. Add garlic and fry until brown, then remove from pan and set aside. Add the artichokes and fry for 5 minutes, add the red pepper flakes and fry for one more minute. Add the lemon juice and beef stock, and simmer until the artichokes are tender.
    Garnish individual servings with the toasted garlic.
    Serves 6

Artichoke soup

Now you have the Californians in your grasp. But they are a clever lot, and not easily fooled. Unless you wine them well. No matter where you are in the wine world, you will be able to find the wines of the Golden State. If you are outside California, they will be suckers for zinfandel, if for no other reason than they are away from home and long for its taste. What could be more understandable? Pour them a bit of zin and they are yours.

Now whether you are within or without California, you must serve a salad. It really doesn't matter what type, as long as it's not a wedge of iceberg lettuce slathered with Thousand Island Dressing. Maybe you can get away with that in New York, but not here, unless it's as a gastronomic joke, which will happen from time to time. If you see it, laugh and move on. A Caesar (see p35) or any other tossed salad is fine. At Chez Panisse, a favorite is a toss of thinly sliced celery and fennel bulb dressed with a mild vinaigrette and dusted with shavings of dry cheese. Don't go for the Crab Louis (see p40) or Cobb salad (see p38) as they are dinner salads, rather than openers of the appetite. So now what? It depends on where you are and the time of year. Whether you are in California or not, remember that California Cuisine is an idea, a method. It depends on the season and the region. You can be in Australia, or even in the UK, and still produce something of which Californians can say "this tastes like home."

Roast Pork with Mission Figs

If figs are out of season you can use dates, and lamb can be substituted for pork.

Ingredients

1	pork butt (deboned pork shoulder), 4–5 lbs (2–2¼ kg)
1 tbs	brandy or sherry
6	ripe mission figs, quartered lengthwise
2 tbs	fresh sage, finely chopped
2 tbs	fresh garlic, finely chopped
2 tsp	ground black pepper
1 tsp	salt
12	whole cloves

Preheat the oven to 350°F (175°C). Place the meat in an ovenproof baking dish. Rub the inside of the meat with the brandy or sherry, and fill with the figs. Truss the meat with kitchen twine. Rub the outside with the sage, garlic, pepper, and salt. Push the cloves into the outside of the meat. Roast for 40 to 45 minutes per pound.

Serves 8

Roast pork with mission figs

You'll need olive oil. Maybe unsalted butter. And you'll need good bread. Unless you're entertaining vegetarians the centerpiece of your meal will be the meat course. A pork (or lamb) roast stuffed with native fruit and tarted up with local wine will get you kudos aplenty. Mission figs are one of the earliest cultivated crops in California, having been introduced with the Spanish missionaries, so you'll be serving a bit of history on the side. Such a dish would be well accompanied by a creamy polenta or a wild rice pilaf. Golden Staters are silly for sautéed snow peas, and their vivid green would contrast well with the gold of polenta.

For a sweet at the end you can never go wrong with fruit. While they take it fresh and unadorned during the day, Californians like it slightly altered when part of a more formal repast. Not too altered, though, just enough to show a bit of creativity. So try blood oranges with herb and honey syrup.

Blood Oranges with Herb & Honey Syrup

Ingredients

9	blood oranges
¼ cup	honey
¼ cup	water
1 tsp	fresh pungent herb (eg, rosemary, sage, thyme, saffron)

Using a sharp knife, remove the peel and pith from the oranges. Slice the oranges thinly crosswise and arrange them in a serving dish. Combine the honey, water, and herb in a small saucepan over medium heat and bring to the boil, stirring. Cover, remove from the heat, and allow it to steep for 15 minutes. Strain the mixture and drizzle it over the oranges.

Garnish with your herb of choice.

Serves 6

Californian honey

A

abalone 65-6
Acme bakery 73, 141
alcohol
  beer 105-8, 198
  cocktails 109-15, 194
  drink driving 193
  wine 82-104
American Viticultural Areas
  (AVAs) 97
Anaya, Señor Ignacio 206
artichoke 41, 209
Auberge du Soleil 94-5
avocado 50-1

B

bakers, artisanal 74-5
Banducci, Enrico 139
banquets 205-14
bar & grills 190-1
Bar Tosca 113
barbecues 129-31
bars, see places to drink; restaurants, cafés, and bars
Bauer, Linda-Marie 47
Bay Area 139
Beard, James 14
beef 53-6
beer 105-8, 198
Benchley, Robert 109
Bergeron, "Trader Vic" 142
Berkeley 16, 29
Berkeley Farmers' Market 176-7
Bertolli, Paul 22
Bierce, Ambrose 64, 67, 156, 196
Big Stone Lodge 130
biscuits & gravy 166
blood oranges 212
Bonaventure Hotel 153, 187
bookings 23-8
Boudin, Isidore 142

bread 73
  artisanal bakers 74-5
brewpubs 107-8, 198
Bristol Farms Market 152
Brown Derby 39
Bryce, James 40
Buena Vista Cafe 112
Burbank, Luther 142
burritos 156-8

C

Cadillac Desert 18
Caesar salad 35-7
California Cuisine 21-8
California Culinary Academy 30
Californios 12, 83
Cal-Mex cuisine 125-6, 150-1,
  206-7
cantinas 200
Cardini, Caesar 35-7
Carneros 94-5
Carrara's Cafe 141, 169-70
Carroll, Lewis 65
Carson, Kit 56
Casa Orinda 165
celebrations 127-35, see also
  festivals
Central Coast Counties 104
Central Valley 18-19
Central Valley Counties 103
Chasen, Dave 56
Chasen's 56, 130, 152
cheese 69-80
  Monterey Jack 70-1
Chez Panisse 16, 21-2, 141, 143,
  183-5
chicken 66
Child, Julia 14
children
  cooking courses 29-30
  dining with 28

chile 54-6
chile con carne 54-6, 146-7, 150-1
Chilean sea bass 61, 188
chilli, *see* chile
Chinatown 140, 153
Chinese Kitchen 142
chocolate 79
chop suey 126
CIA (Culinary Institute of
    America) 30, 91
cioppino 148-9
Cobb, Bob 39
Cobb salad 38-9
cocktails 109-15, 194
    Irish coffee 112-13
    mai tai 142
    margarita 114-15
    martini 109-12
coffee 116-17
Compass Rose 111
cooking
    car 167-70
    home 121-6
    ingredients 123
COPIA 87
corkage 26, 93
country & western bars 201
Cowgirl Creamery 22, 69-70
Coyote Cafe 22
Crab Louis 40
Crossroads Café 185
Culhane, Garrett 19, 179
culture 9-30

D
DeGroot, Roy Andres 148
Delancey Street Restaurant 184-5
Delaplane, Stanton 113
desserts 78-80, 211-12
dining out, *see* places to eat

drinks 81-120, *see also* alcohol
    coffee 116-17
    juice 120
    tea 117-18
    water 119
duck 66-7
Dungeness crab 40, 148

E
Earthbound Farm 30
eating habits 21-8
Edible Schoolyard 29, 141
El Camino Real 11-12
El Cholo Cafe 132, 151
enology 87
Enrico's 139-40
Epperson, Frank 142
etiquette 23-8

F
fast food 17
festivals
    Gilroy Garlic Festival 133-5
    harvest festivals 133-5
Fior D'Italia 139
fish 59-61
    Chilean sea bass 61, 188
    Pacific halibut 61
    salmon 60, 169
    sand dabs 146-7
Fisher, Mary Frances
    Kennedy 14-15
Fisherman's Wharf 140
Flabob Airport Cafe 166
Fong-Torres, Shirley 172-3
Four Seasons Hotel 152
Fourth Street 141
49ers 12, 62-3
fortune cookies 80, 173

Fragrant Vegetable 204
French Laundry 94-5
French-dip sandwich 158
fruits 48-50
    blood oranges 212
    Meyer lemon 49

G
Gadsby, Robert 154
Gallo 88-9
Garden Project, The 184
garlic 133-5
gay bars 200
geography 11, 18
ghost towns 62-3
Gillespie, Elgy 185
Gilroy Garlic Festival 133-5
Gold Rush 12, 84
Gourmet Ghetto 141
Grand Central Market 153, 174
grass shrimp 63
gratuity 27
Greens Restaurant 204
guacamole 50-1

H
Hangtown fry 143-5
Harazthy, Count 84
Harris' 187
Hechinger, Charles 22
Heinold's First and Last Chance
    Saloon 139, 141
Henry's World Famous Hi-Life
    130
herbs 44-7
history 10-16, 130
hot fudge sundae 78
Hotel del Coronado 196
House of Prime Rib 187

I
ice cream 78
influences
    Asian 22
    Chinese 13, 62-3, 126, 172-3
    French 14
    Italian 13
    Mexican 13, 54-6, 125-6,
      156-8, 162-3, 174, 200,
      206-7
    Spanish 11-12, 83, 132
Irish coffee 112-13
It's It, the 78

J
Jack London Square 141
Jack's 139
John's Grill 139
Jordan, Michelle Anna 15, 157
juice 120

K
Kerouac, Jack 139
Khan, Johnny 142
Kuleto, Pat 94

L
LA Four Seasons Hotel 194
La Frontera (The Frontier) 161
LA Prime 187
lamb 57
Lenkert, Erika 27
London broil 54
London, Jack 139

M
McCarty, Michael 22
McDonald, Paula 163

INDEX

margarita 114-15
markets 171-80
    Berkeley Farmers' Market 176-7
    Briston Farms Market 152
    Chinatown 140, 153
    farmers' markets 140, 152,
    174-5
    Grand Central Market 153,
    174
Martini House 94-5
Martuni's 194
masa 157
Mathieu, Philippe 158
Maytag, Fritz 106
Mendocino County 101
Mexican influences 13, 54-6,
    125-6, 156-8, 162-3, 174,
    200, 206-7
Meyer lemon 49
microgreens 154
Mike's Time Out Restaurant and
    Lounge 166
Millennium 204
Millennium Biltmore
    Hotel 153-4, 196
Miller, Jason 148
Miller, Laurel 177
Miller, Mark 22
mission grape 83
missionaries 11-13
Montalvo, Garcia Ordoñez de 10
Monterey Jack 70-1
Moose, Ed & Mary Etta 146-7
Moose's Restaurant 147
music bars 201
Musso & Frank Grill 151-2

N
nachos 206-7
Napa County 100

Napa Valley 83
Northern California 139-48
nuts 48

O
Occidental Hotel site 140
olive oil 77
Olivera Street 153
olives 77
Oliveto 22
oysters 62-5

P
Pacific 22
Pacific halibut 61
Pacific Rim (PacRim) cuisine 22
Palace Hotel 196
parking 25-8
Peet, Alfred 116-17
Peet's Coffee & Tea 116-17, 141
Philippe the Original 153, 158
Placerville 143-5
places to drink 193-201, see also
    alcohol
    brewpubs 107-8, 198
    cocktail lounges 194
    hotel bars 196-7
    saloons 199
    theme bars 199-201
    trains 197
    wine bars 195
places to eat 183-91
    bar & grills 190-1
    California Cuisine 183-5
    Italian 139
    roadhouses 165-6
    seafood houses 188-9
    steak houses 186-7
    vegan 203-4
    vegetarian 203-4

pork 57, 210
Porter, William Sydney 142
Prohibition era 35-7, 82, 85-6
Project Open Hand 184
pubs 201
Puck, Wolfgang 21-2, 155

R
Rainwater's on Kettner 187
ranchos 12
Red Room 194
regions 137-70
    Northern California 139-48
    Southern California 150-9
    wine regions 97-104
reservations 23-8
restaurants, cafés, and bars
    Auberge du Soleil 94-5
    Bar Tosca 113
    Big Stone Lodge 130
    Buena Vista Cafe 112
    Carneros 94-5
    Carrara's Cafe 141, 169-70
    Casa Orinda 165
    Chasen's 56, 130
    Chez Panisse 16, 21-2, 141,
        143, 183-5
    Compass Rose 111
    Cowgirl Creamery 22, 69-70
    Coyote Cafe 22
    Crossroads Café 185
    Delancey Street Restaurant
        184-5
    El Cholo Cafe 132, 151
    Enrico's 139-40
    Flabob Airport Cafe 166
    Fragrant Vegetable 204
    French Laundry 94-5
    Greens Restaurant 204
    Harris' 187

    Heinold's First and Last
        Chance Saloon 139, 141
    Henry's World Famous Hi-
        Life 130
    House of Prime Rib 187
    Jack's 139
    John's Grill 139
    LA Prime 187
    Martini House 94-5
    Martuni's 194
    Mike's Time Out Restaurant
        and Lounge 166
    Millennium 204
    Moose's Restaurant 147
    Musso & Frank Grill 151-2
    Oliveto 22
    Pacific 22
    Rainwater's on Kettner 187
    Red Room 194
    Saloon, The 139-40
    Spago 21-3
    Stars Restaurant 22
    Tadich Grill 139-40
    ThirstyBear Brewing
        Company 107-9, 140
road trips 164
Road, the 164-70
roadhouses 165-6

S
Saint Francis Hotel 111, 140
salad 35-40
    Caesar salad 35-7
    Cobb salad 38-9
    Crab Louis 40
salmon 60, 169
saloons 199
Saloon, The 139-40
San Antonio Winery 153
sand dabs 146-7

INDEX

Santa Clara County 102
Santa Maria barbecue 156
sausage 58
seafood houses 188-9
Serra, Father Junipero 11, 83
shellfish
    abalone 65-6
    Dungeness crab 40
    grass shrimp 63
    oysters 62-5
    spiny lobster 159
shopping 171-80, *see also* markets
    walking tours 172
Sierra Foothills Counties 103
Smith, Peggy 22
smoking 26
Snow, Jack 165
Solano Avenue 141
Sonoma 12
Sonoma County 101
Sonoma Valley 83
Southern California 150-9
Spago 21-2
Spanish influences 11-12, 83, 132
spiny lobster 159
sports bars 200
staples 31-80
    artichoke 41
    avocado 50-1
    beef 53-6
    bread 73
    cheese 69-80
    chicken 66
    duck 66-7
    fish 59-61
    herbs 44-7
    lamb 57
    Meyer lemon 49
    olive oil 77
    olives 77

pork 57, 210
salad 35-40
sausage 58
shellfish 62-6
sweets 78-80
tomato 43
turkey 67-80
Starbucks 117
Stars Restaurant 22
steak houses 186-7
steam beer 105-7
Stevenson, Robert Louis 85
Strauss, Levi 144
Stuart Street 140
Sullivan, Steve 73
Sustainable Kitchen, The 29
sweets 78-80

T

tacos 125-6
Tadich Grill 139-40
tamales 132
tea 117-18
theme bars 199-201
ThirstyBear Brewing
    Company 107-8, 140
Thomas, Jerry 109
tipping 27
tomato 43
tortillas 157
Tower, Jeremiah 22
traditions 121-6
Tschelitscheff, Andre 91
turkey 67-80
Twain, Mark 12

U

University of California 87
utensils 123

V
Vallejo, General Mariano 12, 84
vegan 203-4
vegetables 33-43
vegetarian 203-4

W
water, bottled 119
Waters, Alice 16, 21-2, 29
Westin Bonaventure Hotel 194
Westin Saint Francis 196
wine 82-104
    bars 195
    corks 95
courses 87
history 82-93
mission grape 83
regions 97-104
tastings 93
varieties 97-104
Wine Country Trail 94-5
Wok Wiz Walking Tours and
    Cooking 173

Z
Zappa, Frank 105
zinfandel grape 84

Boxed Text
A Civilized Sip 197
A Little Ignacio, Please 206-7
A Matter of Convenience 17
Berkeley Farmers' Market 176-7
Bootlegger 82
By the Glass 90
California Culinary
    Councilor 136
Central Valley Native Son 19
Continuing Education 29, 87
Corkage 93
Don't Miss
    La Frontera 161
    Northern California 142
    Road, The 164
    Southern California 159
Faces of Gastronomy
    M. F. K. Fisher 15
    Mr. Greens 154
    Saloon Lord, The 146-7
    Village Baker, The 74-5
Felons & Fodder 184-5
Getting Tipsy 27
Ghostly Fare? 62-3
Herbal Renaissance 44-7
How My Butcher Changed My
    Palate 178-9
Screw You? 95
Take a Bow 84
Through the Glass Blurry 162-3
Walrus and the Carpenter, The 65
Warning Label 101
Wine to Go 86
Wraps Rant 157

Maps
California 6-7
Legend 2
Los Angeles 150
    Downtown & Chinatown 153
    Hollywood 152
    Koreatown 152
Regions 138
San Francisco Bay Area 139
    Berkeley 141
    Oakland 141
    San Francisco 140
Wine Country Trail 94
Wine Regions 98-9

Recipes

Artichoke Soup 211
Blood Oranges with Herb and Honey Syrup 214
Brown Derby Dessing 39
Caesar Salad 37
Cioppino 149
Cobb Salad 38
Guacamole 51
Hangtown Fry 144
Irish Coffee 113
Roast Pork with Mission Figs 212
Salmon Steaks with Pepper, Meyer Lemon & Haricots Verts 169

MORE WORLD FOOD TITLES

Brimming with cultural insight, the World Food series takes the guesswork out of new cuisines and provides the ideal guide to your own culinary adventures. These books cover the full spectrum of food and drink in each country – the history and evolution of the cuisine, its staples & specialities, and the kitchen philosophy of the people.

You'll find definitive two-way dictionaries, menu readers, useful phrases for shopping, drunken apologies, and much more.

The World Food series is the essential guide for traveling and non-traveling food lovers across the globe.

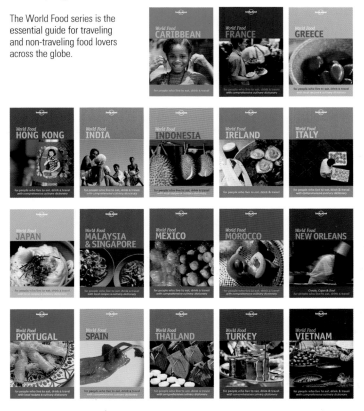

The Lonely Planet Story

Lonely Planet published its first book in 1973 in response to the numerous "How did you do it?" questions Maureen and Tony Wheeler were asked after driving, bussing, hitching, sailing, and railing their way from England to Australia. Written at a kitchen table and hand collated, trimmed, and stapled, Across Asia on the Cheap became an instant local bestseller.

Eighteen months in South-East Asia resulted in their second guide, South-East Asia on a Shoestring, which they put together in a backstreet Chinese hotel in Singapore in 1975. The "yellow bible", as it quickly became known to backpackers around the world, soon became the guide to the region. It has sold well over $^3/_4$ million copies and is now in its 10th edition, still retaining its familiar yellow cover.

Today there are over 400 titles, including travel guides, walking guides, language kits & phrasebooks, travel atlases & maps, diving guides, first time travel guides, condensed guides, illustrated pictorials, and travel literature. The company is the largest independent travel publisher in the world.

The emphasis continues to be on travel for independent travelers. Tony and Maureen still travel for several months of each year and play an active part in the writing, updating, and quality control of Lonely Planet's guides.

They have been joined by over 120 authors and over 400 staff at our offices in Melbourne (Australia), Oakland (USA), London (UK), and Paris (France). Travelers themselves also make a valuable contribution to the guides through the feedback we receive in thousands of letters each year and on our web site.

The people at Lonely Planet strongly believe that travelers can make a positive contribution to the countries they visit, both through their appreciation of the countries' culture, wildlife, and natural features, and through the money they spend. In addition, the company makes a direct contribution to the countries and regions it covers. Since 1986 a percentage of the income from each book has been donated to ventures such as famine relief in Africa; aid projects in India; agricultural projects in Central America; and Greenpeace's efforts to halt French nuclear testing in the Pacific.

Lonely Planet Offices

Australia
90 Maribyrnong St, Footscray, Victoria, 3011
☎ 03 8379 8000
fax 03 8379 8111
email: talk2us@lonelyplanet.com.au

USA
150 Linden St, Oakland, CA 94607
☎ 510 893 8555 TOLL FREE: 800 275 8555
fax 510 893 8572
email: info@lonelyplanet.com

UK
10a Spring Place, London NW5 3BH
☎ 020 7428 4800
fax 020 7428 4828
email: go@lonelyplanet.co.uk

France
1 rue du Dahomey, 75011 Paris
☎ 01 55 25 33 00
fax 01 55 25 33 01
email: bip@lonelyplanet.fr